Principles of Agricultural Economics and Farm Management

NIPA® GENX ELECTRONIC RESOURCES & SOLUTIONS P. LTD.
New Delhi-110 034

About the Authors

Dr. H.L. Singh awarded Ph.D. degree in Dairy Economics from National Dairy Research Institute (NDRI) Karnal (HRY) in 2001. He has experience of 25 years in teaching and research in the discipline at different positions like Assistant professor, Senior Scientist (at ZPD Zone -3 Umium, Barapani), Associate Professor and Professor. He is presently working as Head, Department of Agricultural Economics, College of Agriculture, SVPUA&T Meerut and actively involved in policy issues at state and national level. He has awarded with several awards and honors by various societies during previous service period. He has edited and authored text book in his area of specialization. He has 52 research articles and 12 popular article, book chapters etc. in his credit.

Dr. Supriya is presently working as Associate Professor in the Department of Agricultural Economics Acharya Narendra Deva University of Agriculture and Technology, Ayodhya (U.P.) She has completed her Doctorate Degree in Agricultural Economics from G.B.P.U A & T, Pantnagar in year 2009 and qualified ARS Net in Economics and Agribusiness Management. She has also done Post Graduate Diploma in Business Management with Human Resources as specialization from SCDL, Pune and M.A. Economics from Kumaon University. She has received University Fellowship during Master's and Doctoral Program.

She has varied experience in the fields of research and teaching while working at IARI, New Delhi and Teaching at G.B.P.U.A&T, Pantnagar.

She has more than 86 Research articles published in reputed NAAS rated and other peer reviewed journals. She wrote Book on "Farm Management and its Practical Utility", "Agribusiness Fundamentals of Decision Making", "Manual Cum Workbook on Agricultural Finance & Cooperation", "Farm Management, Production & Resource Economics", "Agricultural Finance & Cooperation", "Fundamental of Agribusiness Management & Intellectual Property Rights". In collaboration with Extension and Statistics Fellows also contributed Book chapters and book in the area of Extension Education and Agricultural Statistics. She has also written many popular articles published in Hindi and English Magazines. She has also received Excellence awards by many societies in the area of Research and Teaching like Young Scientist award and Excellence in Teaching. She has taught various courses at Undergraduate and Post Graduate level. Her area of specialization is Agricultural Economics with Agricultural statistics as minor.

Dr. Rajani Gautam, D/O Shri Girish Gautam and Smt. Lalita Gautam was born on 09 July, 1982. Dr. Rajani Gautam is presently working as an Assistant Professor in Department of Commerce, Pandit Shambhu Nath Shukla University, Shahdol, Madhya Pradesh, India. Author is having 17 year teaching experience (UG, PG and Ph.D. students). She published 20 research paper in peer-reviewed National and International Scopus journal and three books published by reputed publisher. She had 15 year teaching experience in Thukur Ranmat Singh College NAAC A+ Rewa (M.P.).

Dr. Pradeep Mishra, is an Assistant Professor of Statistics at the College of Agriculture, Rewa at the Jawaharlal Nehru Krishi Vishwa Vidyalaya, Madhya Pradesh, India. During his PhD research work, he was selected for an INSPIRE Fellowship by the Department of Science and Technology of the Government of India. Dr. Mishra has served as a data management specialist at a private multinational company for several years. His area of specialization is agriculture statistics, time series, and design of experiment. He has published more than 141 research articles in different international and national journals. Also, he won several awards, including an award for young scientists in at an international conference (GRISAAS-2017); best doctoral degree in 2018 at an international conference on advances in agriculture and allied science technologies for sustainable development, in Hyderabad, a second best paper award from the Society of Economics & Development in PAU. 2018, among others. Dr. Mishra earned his B.Sc. in Agriculture from the College of Agriculture, Bilaspur, affiliated with the Indira Gandhi Krishi Vishwavidyalaya, Raipur (C.G.); his MSc in Agricultural Statistics from the College of Agriculture, Jawaharlal Nehru Agricultural University; and his PhD in Agriculture Statistics, specializing in modeling and forecasting of foods crops in India and their yield sustainability.

Dr. Aditya Bhooshan Srivastava is presently working as a Guest faculty in the Department of Agricultural Economics at the College of Agriculture, Rewa at the Jawaharlal Nehru Krishi Vishwa Vidyalaya, Madhya Pradesh, India. He has completed his Doctorate degree in Agricultural Economics from Acharya Narendra Deva University of Agriculture & Technology, Kumarganj, Ayodhya (U.P.) in 2024. He has also completed his Master degree from Acharya Narendra Deva University of Agriculture & Technology, Kumarganj, Ayodhya in 2021. He has Young Research Award and Best thesis award by agricultural societies. He has 24 research paper in peer review National and International journal. He has also written 14 popular articles and 12 book Chapter. He also wrote Book on "Manual Cum Workbook on Agricultural Finance & Cooperation", "Farm Management, Production & Resource Economics", "Agricultural Finance & Cooperation".

Principles of Agricultural Economics and Farm Management

H.L. Singh
Professor
Department of Agricultural Economics
SVP University of Agriculture and Technology
Meerut, Uttar Pradesh

Supriya
Associate Professor
Department of Agricultural Economics
A.N.D. University of Agriculture and Technology
Ayodhya, Uttar Pradesh

Rajani Gautam
Assistant Professor
Department of Commerce
Pandit Shambhu Nath Shukla University
Shahdol, Madhya Pradesh

Pradeep Mishra
Assistant Professor
Department of Agricultural Statistics
College of Agriculture, Rewa
Jawaharlal Nehru Krishi Vishwavidyalaya
Jabalpur, Madhya Pradesh

Aditya Bhooshan Srivastava
Guest Faculty
Department of Agricultural Economics
College of Agriculture, Rewa
Jawaharlal Nehru Krishi Vishwavidyalaya
Jabalpur, Madhya Pradesh

NIPA® GENX ELECTRONIC RESOURCES & SOLUTIONS P. LTD.
New Delhi-110 034

NIPA® GENX ELECTRONIC RESOURCES & SOLUTIONS P. LTD.

101,103, Vikas Surya Plaza, CU Block
L.S.C.Market, Pitam Pura, New Delhi-110 034
Ph. +91 11 27341616, 27341717, 27341718
E-mail: newindiapublishingagency@gmail.com
www: www.nipabooks.com

For customer assistance, please contact
Phone: + 91-11-27 34 17 17
Fax: + 91-11-27 34 16 16
E-Mail: feedbacks@nipabooks.com

Print ISBN: 978-93-58874-30-3

ebook ISBN: 978-93-58879-55-1

Composed and Designed by NIPA®.

Preface

Agriculture is the backbone of economies worldwide, feeding nations and fueling growth. Yet, its success hinges on a delicate balance of economic principles and effective management practices. Principal of Agricultural Economics and Farm Management is crafted to unravel this intricate relationship, offering a roadmap to understanding the forces that shape agricultural productivity and sustainability.

This book takes you on a journey through the core concepts of agricultural economics, from the fundamentals of demand, production, and cost to the complexities of national income, international trade, and the Goods and Services Tax (GST). It delves into the laws of returns, input-output relationships, and the dynamics of supply and distribution, providing both theoretical insights and practical applications. With a focus on agricultural planning and development, it also addresses pressing global issues like population growth, economic systems, and balance of payments.

Whether you are a student, researcher, or practitioner, this book is designed to equip you with the knowledge and tools to navigate the challenges of modern agriculture. By blending theory with real-world relevance, it aims to inspire innovative thinking and sustainable solutions. Let this book be your guide to mastering the art and science of agricultural economics and farm management.

Authors

Contents

1

Economics

1.1. What is Economics?

If we see our day-to-day activities, most of which are related to earning one's own living and to the manner of satisfying one's own wants. These human activities, which are generally called economic, are mainly related to production, distribution, consumption and exchange of goods and services. ***The scientific study of various problems arising out of these economic activities is called economics***.

1.2. Basic Economic Problem

The basic economic problem is **Human wants are many; but means to satisfy these wants are limited.** These limited means are capable of alternative uses and hence there is a need of satisfying maximum wants with limited resources. In reality most resources are scarce. Similarly, Individuals and nations possess boundless desires, yet they are constrained by a finite pool of resources, including labor, machinery, factories, and raw materials. These scarce resources can be allocated in multiple ways to fulfill various needs. Likewise, individuals have limited financial means but an array of wants they aspire to satisfy, necessitating careful decision-making regarding resource utilization.

For instance, a farmer has the option to cultivate crops such as paddy, sugarcane, banana, or cotton on his garden land. However, the choice of crop must be made based on the availability of irrigation water, as different crops have varying water requirements. More example are shown in figure 1.

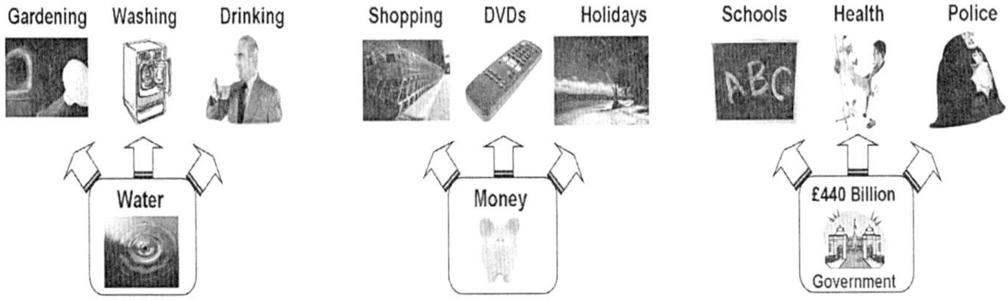

Fig. 1: Basic Economics Problem

1.3. Circle of Economics

The foundation of all economic activity lies in the existence of human wants. To fulfill these wants, effort is essential, as they cannot be satisfied without deliberate action. Thus, the interplay between wants, efforts, and satisfaction creates a continuous cycle that drives economic activity.

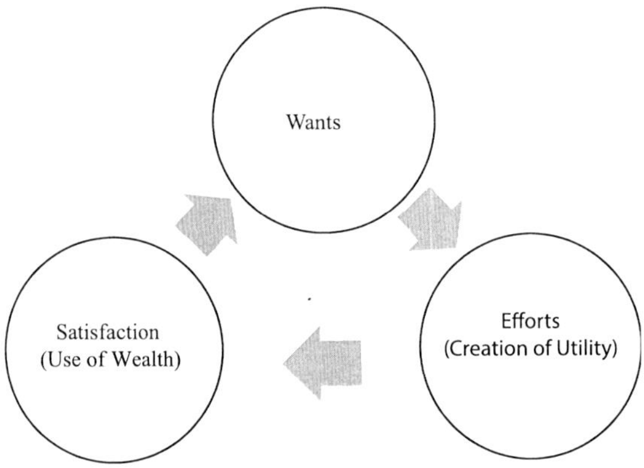

1.4. Definitions of Economics

The word economics has been derived from the Greek word "*OIKONOMICAS*" with "*OIKOS*" meaning a household and "*NOMOS*" meaning management. It is understood that the beginning was made by the Greek Philosopher, Aristotle who in his book "*Economica*" focused that the field of economics deals with household management.

The economists in defining the term, economics, followed several approaches and concepts. The concepts on which various definitions of economics given are: **Wealth, Welfare, Scarcity, and Growth.**

1.4.1. "Wealth" Definition by Adam Smith

Adam Smith (1723-90) in his book entitled "*Wealth of Nations*" (1776) defined economics as ***"An enquiry into the nature and causes of wealth of nations"***. He is regarded as the "***Father of Economics***" because he was the first person who put all the economic ideas in a systematic way. It is only after Adam Smith; we study economics as a systematic science.

The term "wealth" carries distinct meaning in Economics. While in everyday language "wealth", we mean money, but in economics, wealth refers to those goods which satisfy human wants. We regard only those items that are relatively rare and possess monetary worth as riches. We examine the consumption, production, exchange, and distribution of wealth..

Criticism

Smith defined economics exclusively in terms of wealth, not in terms of human welfare. Ruskin and Carlyle condemned economics as a "dismal science" because it taught selfishness, which was incompatible with ethics. Nevertheless, wealth is now regarded as a means to an end, with the ultimate goal being human welfare. Consequently, the wealth definition was rejected, and the focus has shifted from "wealth" to "welfare'.

1.4.2. "Welfare" Definition by Alfred Marshall

Alfred Marshall (1842-1924) wrote a book "*Principles of Economics*" in 1890. According to him ***"Economics is a study of man's actions in the ordinary business of life; it inquires how he gets his income and how he uses it".***

Marshall agrees that economics studies about wealth. But he does not accept the view that economics studies about wealth alone. In the words of Marshall, "Economics is on the one side a study of wealth, and on the other and more important side, a part of the study of man. Man is the center of his study. According to him, the study of man is more important than the study of wealth. Wealth is sought only for promoting human welfare. Hence wealth is given a secondary position.

Marshall's definition is known as material welfare definition of economics because of its emphasis on welfare. **Welfare is the well-being of individual**

or community. This definition by Marshal remained current for a long time, but early in the 1930's, a distinguished economist Lionel Robbins challenged the definition as under. –

- Economics was treated as a social science rather than a human science; and the term "human science" is more apt on the ground that any individual either as a member of society or in isolation does have economic problems.
- It classifies economic phenomena into material and non-material; and it ignores the non-material services like those of teachers, doctors etc. which also make an important contribution to economic welfare.

Criticism

a) Marshall's definition of economics primarily considers material goods, overlooking the significance of immaterial services such as those provided by doctors and teachers. However, these services play a crucial role in enhancing societal welfare and should not be excluded from economic analysis.

b) Marshall differentiates between (i) goods and services that contribute to human welfare and (ii) those that do not. However, economics also encompasses commodities like liquor, which, despite lacking a direct welfare-enhancing function, possess market value and are subject to economic analysis.

c) Marshall's definition is centred on the concept of welfare, yet the term lacks a universally accepted definition. Welfare is a dynamic concept, varying across individuals, nations, and time periods. Broadly, it refers to the well-being or quality of life of individuals and societies. The welfare of a person or a nation is not solely determined by the accumulation of wealth but is also influenced by political stability, social structures, and cultural factors.

1.4.3. "Scarcity" Definition by Lionel Robbins

Lionel Robbins (1898-1984) has defined economics as follows: ***"Economics is the science which studies human behavior as a relationship between ends and scarce means which have alternative uses"***. Robbins has given the above definition in his book *"An Essay on the Nature and significance of Economic Science"*. The definition of Robbins is based on the following basic assumptions.

- Ends are various. The term “ends” mean wants. Human wants are unlimited.
- Means are limited. Means like time, money and resources are limited.
- We can put means to alternative uses. For example, though time is limited, we can use it for different purposes. We can use time for earning money or we may enjoy it as leisure, and
- All wants are not of equal importance.

We know time is limited. There are only 24 hours in a day. If a worker wants only money he has to work for long hours and forgo leisure. If he wants leisure, he has to forgo his income. He cannot have both at the same time. We may, however, note that all means which satisfy human wants are not limited. For example, air and sunshine are available in abundance. They are free goods. But many things we want are scarce in relation to our wants.

So, economics studies human behaviour as a relationship between unlimited wants and scarce means. As means are limited, we have to pay a price for them. We study in economics how the prices of scarce goods are determined. We have to choose among different wants. That is why we say that **scarcity** and **choice** are central problems in economics

Robbins’s definition is superior to “wealth” and “welfare” definitions because ‘welfare’ aspect is embodied in the definition and ‘wealth’ is represented as means which is always scare.

Criticism

a) Robbins does not differentiate between goods that enhance human welfare and those that do not. Both rice and alcoholic beverages require scarce resources for their production, yet while rice contributes positively to human well-being, alcoholic beverages may not. Despite this, Robbins asserts that economics remains neutral regarding the desirability of different ends.

b) Economics encompasses both microeconomic and macroeconomic dimensions, analyzing resource allocation, price determination, and broader issues such as national income generation. However, Robbins’ definition narrows the scope of economics primarily to the theory of resource allocation, overlooking its broader macroeconomic aspects.

c) Robbins’ definition is limited in scope as it does not account for the theories of economic growth and development, which are essential components of economic analysis.

1.4.4. "Growth" Definition by Lord Keynes

During the last 40 years or so, economic thinking has moved further from Robbins's view. The credit for bringing about a revolution in economic thinking goes to Lord Keynes (1883-1946). He defined economics as "*the study of the administration of scare resources and of the determinants of employment and income*". Consequently, Economics investigates the mechanisms by which the levels of income and employment in an economy are established, in addition to the allocation of resources. In other words, it also investigates the causes of economic fluctuations to determine how economic stability can be enhanced.

The major implications of this definition are as follows:

a) Samuelson introduces a dynamic approach by adding the temporal aspect, therefore embracing the theory of economic growth within the realm of economics.

b) He emphasises the main issue of lack in a world where people want everything. Resources are limited and can be used in many different ways, so they need to be distributed efficiently.

c) His formulation encompasses the basic economic functions—production, distribution, and consumption—and provides a holistic framework for economic study.

Of all the definitions discussed above, the 'growth' definition stated by Samuelson appears to be the most satisfactory.

Economics is, therefore, appropriately regarded as the examination of the allocation of scarce resources (in relation to unlimited purposes) and the determinants of income, output, employment, and economic growth.

1.5. Scope of Economics

Scope refer to the province or field of study. When discussing the scope of economics, we must indicate whether it is a science, an art, a positive science or a normative science.

i) Economics - A Science or an Art

a) **Economics is a science:** Science is a systematized body of knowledge that traces the relationship between cause and effect. As another thing that science should have, its events should be able to be measured. By looking at these traits, we can say that economics is a field of study where facts have been gathered, sorted, and examined in a planned way.

Economics looks into whether it is possible to draw broad conclusions about why people do the things they do. It is very easy to figure out what people and businesses want by looking at their money. Thus, economics is a science.

b) **Economics is also an art:** An art is a system of rules for the attainment of a given end. A science teaches us to know, whereas art teaches us to do. Applying this definition, we discover that economics provides practical guidance in the resolution of economic problems. Science and art are complementary to each other and economics is both a science and an art.

ii) Economics-Positive or Normative Science

Economics encompasses both positive and normative dimensions. As a positive science, it seeks to explain the "why" and "how" of economic phenomena by analyzing causes and effects. Conversely, as a normative science, it evaluates the rightness or wrongness of the things.

For instance, the statement "12 percent of the labor force in India was unemployed last year" is a positive assertion, as it presents an objective fact that can be empirically verified. In contrast, the claim "12 percent unemployment is too high" is normative, as it involves a value judgment based on a predetermined standard of economic acceptability. Moreover, normative economics goes further by proposing measures to address such issues. Hence, economics functions as both a positive and normative science, explaining economic realities while also assessing their implications and suggesting corrective actions.

Difference between Positive and Normative Economics

As we know that economics is a positive or normative economics are the two different aspects of economics. Positive economic studies the real nature of the subject and normative economics studies the facts not as they are but as they ought to be. So, there are several differences between positive and normative economics which area as follow:-

S.No.	Positive economics	Normative economics
1.	Deals with 'What is' (i.e., describe what exist or how it work)	Deals with what should be or what ought to be
2.	It studies the cause and effect of relationship	It studies the outcome which is right or wrong.
3.	Statement can be empirically verified	Statement may or may not be verified
4.	It deal with how economic problem are solved	It deal with how economic problem should be solved.
5.	It is objective and quantitative in nature	It is subjective and descriptive in nature.
6.	Example: India is over populated country	Example: government should provide basic health care to all.

1.6. Subject-Matter / Divisions of Economics

a) Traditional Approach

The subject matter of economics has traditionally been classified into four fundamental divisions: Consumption, Production, Exchange, and Distribution.

I. **Consumption**: Consumption refers to the utilization of wealth to satisfy a multitude of wants. It also signifies the depletion of utility. All goods that are produced are either consumed immediately or at some point in the future. Essentially, consumption entails the exhaustion of utility as goods are used to fulfill human needs and desires.

II. **Production**: Production is an activity that generates utility by enhancing the usefulness of goods and services. It involves the addition of utility, thereby leading to its definition as the creation of utility. Through the production process, one set of goods is converted into another, wherein inputs are transformed into final products to meet various needs and demands.

III. **Exchange**: In a primitive society, the relationship between wants, efforts, and satisfaction is direct and immediate. When a primitive man feels hungry, he simply picks fruit, consumes it, and satisfies his need. However, in a modern society, this process is far more complex. Individuals produce goods they do not consume and consume goods they do not produce. For instance, a farmer cultivates wheat but cannot utilize it entirely for himself. Instead, he sells it for money, which he then uses to purchase the goods and services he requires. This process of buying and selling is known as exchange.

IV. **Distribution**: Nowadays, most of the goods we require are produced either in fields or factories. Their production involves the contribution of various factors: workers provide labor, landlords supply land, capitalists invest capital, and entrepreneurs coordinate and manage the entire process. Each of these contributors receives a monetary reward for their role—laborers earn wages, landlords receive rent, capitalists gain interest, and entrepreneurs secure profit. Economics examines how these incomes—wages, rent, interest, and profit—are determined, a process known as distribution.

Thus, Consumption, Production, Exchange and Distribution is thc subjcct-matter of economics in traditional view.

b) Modern Approach

The study of economics is divided into: i) Microeconomics and ii) Macroeconomics.

1. **Microeconomics** analyses the economic behavior of individual decision-making units, such as households or firms. It analyzes the flow of economic resources or factors of production from households or resource owners to business firms, as well as the movement of goods and services from firms to households. Additionally, microeconomics explores how individual units determine prices and output levels and how they respond to changes in demand and supply conditions. Due to its focus on price determination, microeconomics is also referred to as price theory.

   Importance of micro economics

   - Helpful in understanding the whole economy
   - Supportive in understanding the working of private sector
   - Helpful in price determination
   - Useful in the formation of economic policies of government
   - Helpful in the study of welfare economics
   - Helpful in formulation of economic laws

2. **Macroeconomics** studies the functioning of the economic system as a whole, encompassing the collective behavior of all decision-making units. It focuses on aggregate measures such as total employment, gross national product (GNP), national income, and the general price level. Due to its emphasis on overall income dynamics, macroeconomics is also referred to as income theory.

Importance of macro-economics:

- Helpful in understanding the working of whole economy.
- Helpful in the formulation of economic policies
- Useful in the study of growth and development
- Helpful in the development of micro economics: it is helpful in testing and development of laws and theories established in micro economics. For ex. The law of diminishing marginal utility could become a law only when it has been tested on the behaviour of certain groups of individual.

1.7. Difference between Micro Economics and Macro Economics

Micro Economics	Macro Economics
It is originated from Greek word MIKROS means small	It is originated from Greek word MAKROS means Large
It studies economy at unit or individual level.	It studies economy as a whole. i.e. at national level.
It includes Consumption, Production, Exchange and Distribution as its subject-matter.	It includes national income, employment, welfare economics, interest, tax, growth etc. as its subject matter.
It is also known as **price theory**.	It is also known as **income theory**.

1.8. Approaches to economic analysis

Static and Dynamic

The term 'statics' originates from the Greek word *statike*, meaning bringing to a standstill. It refers to a state in which movement occurs at a constant level without any variation. In this condition, five key factors remain unchanged: the size of the population, the supply of capital, methods of production, forms of business organization, and the wants of the people. Despite these constants, the economy operates at a steady pace. Static analysis focuses on examining the equilibrium position of the economy under such conditions.

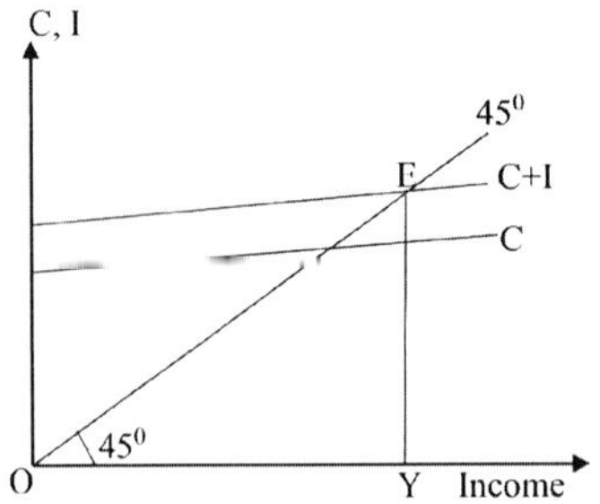

Economic dynamics, in contrast, examines the phenomenon of change within an economy. Over time, an economy may evolve in two distinct ways: (a) maintaining its existing pattern or (b) undergoing a structural transformation. Economic dynamics primarily focuses on the latter. When key factors such as population, capital, production techniques, business organization, or consumer preferences experience shifts—whether individually or collectively—the economic system adapts, leading to a reconfiguration of its structure and direction.

1.9. Nature of Economics

1. **Economics is a social science:** Economics deals with human wants and human behavior and human welfare. Therefore, it is considered as a social science.
2. **Economics is the science of scarcity:** In reality, the resources available to satisfy human wants are limited, leading to scarcity. Both time and money are finite, and essential factors of production—land, labor, and capital—are also constrained. The study of economics arises from this fundamental scarcity, as it seeks to understand how limited resources are allocated to fulfill unlimited desires. Therefore, economics is often described as the science of scarcity, with scarcity itself being a fundamental aspect of life.
3. **Economics is the science of choice:** Human wants are limitless, whereas the resources available to fulfill them are finite, necessitating the process of choice. Although we have numerous desires, not all are equally important. Consequently, we prioritize the most essential and urgent needs. Thus, choice lies at the core of economic activity, making economics fundamentally a science of choice.
4. **Economics studies about the role of money in the affairs of mankind.** The modern economy operates as a monetary economy, where transactions are conducted through money. Prices are expressed in monetary terms, and money facilitates the buying and selling of goods, as well as the payment of rent, wages, interest, and other financial obligations. In economics, we analyze the role of money in shaping human economic activities and interactions.
5. **Economics as a study of the relationship between wealth and welfare**: All scarce goods that fulfill human wants are collectively referred to as wealth. In economics, we examine the production, exchange, distribution, and consumption of wealth. Since wealth is generated to enhance human well-being, economics also explores the relationship between wealth and welfare.

Methodology of Economics

Economics as a science adopts two methods for the discovery of its laws and principles, viz., (a) deductive method and (b) inductive method.

a) **Deductive method:** In this approach, reasoning moves from the general to the specific or particular. It begins with principles that are either self-evident or derived from careful observation and then applies logical reasoning to derive their implicit consequences. For example, the statement "traders earn profit in their businesses" is generally accepted without direct verification from individual traders. The deductive method is particularly valuable in analyzing complex economic phenomena where cause and effect are intricately interwoven. However, its effectiveness depends on the validity of underlying assumptions, such as "traders earn profit if the demand for the commodity is high.

b) **Inductive method:** This method follows an approach that moves from specific or particular observations to general principles. It begins with the examination of particular facts and, through reasoning based on experience, formulates laws and theories derived from observed data. For instance, data on the consumption patterns of low-, middle-, and high-income groups are collected, classified, and analyzed, leading to significant conclusions based on the findings.

The deductive method begins with established principles, either indisputable or derived from rigorous observation, and applies logical reasoning to draw conclusions about specific cases. In contrast, the inductive method examines particular instances to derive general or universal principles. Both methods play a crucial role in economic analysis, complementing each other in understanding economic phenomena.

1.10. Economic Theory

It tries to explain economic phenomena, to interpret why and how the economy behaves and what is the best to solution, how to influence or to solve the economic phenomena. They are comprehensive system of assumptions, hypotheses, definitions and instructions what should be done in a certain economic situation. In principle, the approach to economic theory is divided into positive and normative. All economic theories used to explain specific situations or problems in the economy of some of its models. These models of economic systems try to explain the situation and solve it using approaches that are typical of the economic theory e.g. Keynesian theory subdued stimulates the economy through government money. There are multiple approaches, schools, hypotheses interact and in many ways and often contradict. Economics is not an exact science and how it develops, evolves and changes with the theory. It's about access like politics or philosophy and there never will be the only one true and correct economic theory.

Major Economic Theories

1. **Classical economic theory:** The fundamental principle of the classical theory is that the economy is self-regulating. Classical economists maintain that the economy is always capable of achieving the natural level of real GDP or output, which is the level of real GDP that is obtained when the economy's resources are fully employed.
2. **Keynesian theory:** The economic theories of John M. Keynes who advocate government and fiscal policies intended to stimulate business activity and increase employment.
3. **Monetarism:** The monetarist theory is an economic concept which contends that changes in the money supply are the most significant determinants of the rate of economic growth and the behavior of the business cycle.
4. **New Classical theory:** The neoclassical theory is most widely used economic theory today. You cannot have a meaningful discussion about economics without using the words supply, demand, profit, and satisfaction. The theory was built on foundations laid by classical theorists Adam Smith (1723-1790) and David Ricardo (1772-1823).
5. **New Keynesian theory:** Keynesianism is the various theories about how in the short run and especially during recessions, economic output is strongly influenced by aggregate demand and supply.

Assumption of Economic Rationality

- **The rationality assumption in neoclassical economics:** Almost all of the models studied in traditional economics courses begin with an assumption about the 'rationality' of the parties involved as rational consumers, rational firms and so on. When we usually hear the word rational, we tend to interpret it generally as 'makes well-reasoned decisions.' In an economic context, however, the term has a quite particular meaning. At a high level, we can think of rational consumers as maximizing their long-term utility or happiness and we can think of rational firms as maximizing their long-term profit, but there's a lot more behind the rationality assumption than initially appears.
- **Rational individuals process all information fully, objectively and costlessly:** When consumers attempt to maximize their long-term utility,

what they are actually trying to do is choose from among the multitude of goods and services available for consumption at each point in time. This is no easy task, since doing so requires collecting, organizing, and storing a huge amount of information about the goods available more than we as humans likely have the capacity for. In addition, rational consumers plan for the long term, which is likely impossible to do perfectly in an economy where new goods and services are entering all the time. Furthermore, the assumption of rationality requires that consumers can process all of the necessary information in order to maximize utility without cost.

- **Rational individuals are not subject to framing manipulations:** Since the rationality assumption requires that individuals process information objectively, it implies that individuals are not influenced by the way in information is presented i.e. the 'framing' of the information. Anyone who views 30 percent off and 'pay 70 percent of the original price' as psychologically different, for example, is being affected by the framing of the information.
- **Rational individuals have well-behaved preferences:** In addition, the assumption of rationality requires that an individual's preferences obey certain rules of logic. This doesn't mean, however, that we have to agree with an individual's preferences in order for them to be rational. The first rule of well-behaved preferences is that they are complete and in other words, that when presented with any two goods in the universe of consumption, a rational individual will be able to say which item he or she likes better. This is somewhat difficult when you start to think about how hard to compare goods can be i.e. comparing apples and oranges seems easy once you're asked to determine whether you prefer a kitten or a bicycle.
- **Rational individuals have well-behaved preferences:** The second rule of well-behaved preferences is that they are transitive i.e. that they satisfy the transitive property in logic. In this context, it means that if a rational individual prefers goods A to goods B and also prefers goods B to goods C, then the individual will also prefer goods A to goods C. In addition, it means that if a rational individual is indifferent between goods A and goods B and also indifferent between goods B and goods C, the individual will also be indifferent between goods A and goods C.
- **Rational individuals have time-consistent preferences:** In addition, a rational individual has preferences that are what economists call time consistent. While it may be tempting to conclude that time consistent

preferences require that an individual chooses the same goods at all points in time, this is not actually the case. Instead, time consistent preferences require that an individual will find it optimal to follow through on the plans that she made for the future for example, if a time consistent individual decides that it is optimal to consume a cheeseburger next Tuesday, that individual will still find that decision to be optimal when next Tuesday rolls around.

1.11. Economic laws

Economic laws are fundamental principles that regulate human behavior in economic activities. Similar to scientific laws, they are conditional and apply only when specific conditions are met. While formulating economic theories, economists focus on key factors, assuming other influencing variables remain constant.

According to Robbins, economic laws represent uniform patterns governing human behavior in allocating scarce resources to fulfill unlimited wants.

Characteristics of economic laws

1. **Economic laws differ from government laws** – Unlike government laws, which are rigid and enforceable with penalties for violations, economic laws apply only under specific conditions and are not legally binding.
2. **Economic laws reflect general tendencies** – These laws are derived from observed human behavior in response to economic phenomena. They indicate likely patterns rather than absolute certainties.
3. **Economic laws are hypothetical** – They hold true only under certain assumptions and are typically expressed using the principle of ceteris paribus (all other factors remaining constant).
4. **Economic laws are positive, not normative** – They describe economic realities and relationships but do not prescribe how the economy should function.
5. **Some economic laws are axiomatic** – Certain economic principles, such as the Law of Diminishing Marginal Utility (LDMU), are self-evident and universally applicable.
6. Economic laws lack exactness of the laws of science. Marshall said that these are the laws of tide rather than the laws of gravitation.

1.12. Equilibrium

The term equilibrium has been derived from the combination of two words of Latin language ACQUUS+LIBRQA, which means equal and balance. In common usage, the term '*equilibrium*' means the *state of rest*. In economics, the term equilibrium means the state of absence of changes and not the absence of motion.

According to Prof. Stigler: "*Equilibrium is a position from which there is no net tendency to move, we say net tendency to emphasise the fact that it is not necessarily a state of sudden inertia, but may instead represent the cancellation of power sources.*"

According to Prof. JK Mehta: "*Equilibrium in economics denotes the absence of change in movement.*"

Types of equilibrium

- **Stable:** It tends to resume its original position.
- **Unstable:** Original position is never restored.
- **Neutral:** Disturbing forces neither bring it to the original position nor do they drive it further away.
- **Short term:** Economic forces do not get sufficient time to bring complete adjustment. E.g. supply is adjusted to change in demand.
- **Long term:** There is ample time to change even the means of production or resources available. e. g. If demand increased supply is also increased.
- **Partial:** It relates to single individual, consumer, producer or a firm.
- **General:** It relates with multiplicity of variable. It covers all the organizations functioning in the economy.

Determination of equilibrium price

Equilibrium of price is determined at the point at which demand and supply of a commodity are equal. The price so obtained is called equilibrium price and the quantity so determined is called equilibrium quantity. It can be presented with the help of diagram as follows:

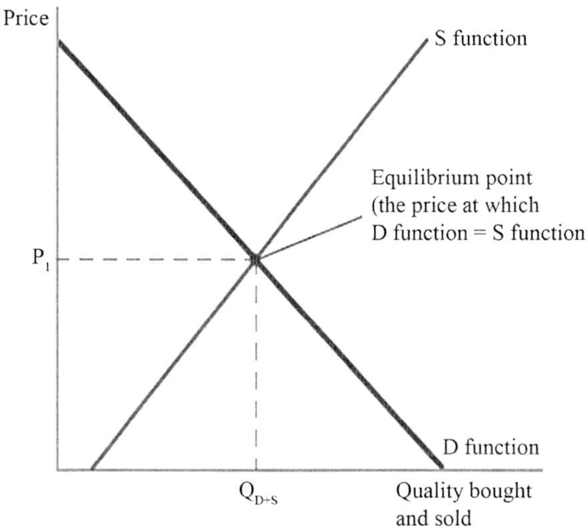

Determination of Equilibrium Price

2

Basic Concept

Every science has its own language. Economics has its own language. There are certain terms which are used in a special sense in economics. So we must understand the meaning of some basic concepts in the field of economics are discussed below.

2.1. Goods

Anything that can satisfies a human want is called a good in economics. For example: Foodgrain, pulse, oilseeds, machinery, seeds, fertilizer, pen, book, etc.

2.2. Services

A service refers to an act or performance that one party provides to another. Services are characterized by their intangible, non-material nature, as well as their inseparability, variability, and perishability. Examples include the services offered by doctors, teachers, lawyers, engineers, and laborers.

Goods	Services
It means the commodities that we use.	It is any act or performance that one party can offer to another.
It is almost always **material**.	It is essentially **non-material**.
It is tangible (goods that can be perceived by sense of touch).	It is intangible (goods which may have value but can not be touched).
It results in ownership.	It does not result in the ownership.
E.g.: land, house, foods, books, cloths, mobile, seeds, fertilizers, etc.	E.g.: the services rendered by doctor, teacher, lawyer, labourers, etc.

2.3. Classification of Goods

Goods are categorized based on four criteria viz., supply, transferability, consumption, and durability as given below:

1. Based on Supply

Goods are classified into economic goods and free goods based on their supply. **Economic goods** are those that require human effort for production and must be purchased at a given price. Their supply is limited relative to demand, and they possess both **value in use** and **value in exchange**. Examples include buildings, machinery, furniture, and various other daily-use items.

In contrast, **free goods** are naturally available in abundance, exceeding demand, and can be obtained without human effort or monetary cost. They have **value in use** but lack **value in exchange**. Common examples include air, sunlight, and rainfall.

However, the distinction between free and economic goods is not always rigid. Under specific circumstances, a free good can become an economic good. For instance, water, which is freely available near rivers and canals, becomes an economic good in areas experiencing water scarcity. Similarly, sand, which is abundant in riverbeds, transforms into an economic good in regions where construction activities require it

- **Difference between economic goods and free goods**

Free Goods	**Economic Goods**
They are the free gifts of nature.	They are produced through human efforts.
No efforts are needed to get it.	Efforts are required to get it.
No price needs to be paid.	They are to be purchased at a given price.
They are **not scarce**.	They are **scare.**
Its supply is more than demand and one can get to the extent they need.	Their supply is less than demand.
They have value-in-use but no value-in-exchange.	They have value in use and value-in- exchange.
E.g.: air, sunlight, rainfall, etc.	E.g.: food, cloth, car, books, etc.

2. Based on Transferability

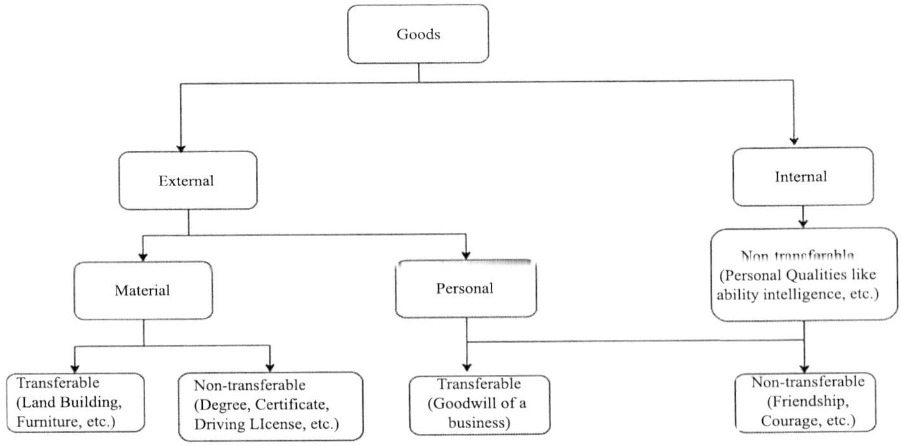

• Difference between Material goods and Non-material goods

Material goods	Non-material goods
The goods which are tangible and concrete are called material goods.	They are various kinds of services. They are intangible, non-material and variable.
e.g.: land, house, foods, books, seeds, cloths, machinery, fertilizers etc.	e.g.: the services rendered by doctor, lawyer, labourer etc.

Difference between Transferable Goods and Non-transferable Goods

Transferable Goods	Non-transferable Goods
They are goods which can change their ownership. They can be physically transferred from one place to other place; however in case of land, physical transfer is not possible, only ownership can be changed.	They are personal qualities which cannot be transferred; only their service can be used by others.
E.g.: car, book, cloths, land, patents, copyright, goodwill of a business, etc.	E.g.: skill, intelligence, degree certificate, driving license, etc.

Difference between Impersonal Goods and Personal Goods

External Goods	Internal Goods
The goods which are not personal, are impersonal goods. They are **what he has**.	They refer to the personal qualities of a person. They are **what he is.**
They are also material and exist outside him, therefore, they are also called **Impersonal Goods.**	They are non-material and exist inside him, therefore, they are also called **Personal Goods.**
E.g.: land, buildings, cloths, etc.	E.g.: ability, skill, knowledge, etc.

Based on Consumption

Based on consumption goods are classified into consumer and producer goods:

Consumer Goods	Producer Goods
They satisfy our wants **directly**.	They are those goods that help to produce other goods. So, they satisfy our wants **indirectly.**
They are also called goods of the **first order** in view of their ability to give direct satisfaction.	They are goods of **second order** in view of their ability to give indirect satisfaction.
They are called **consumption goods.**	They are called **capital good.**
E.g.: food, car, cloths, books, etc.	E.g.: machinery which are used to produce a car, cloth, fertilizers, etc.

Based on Durability

Based on durability the goods are classified into mono-period goods and Poly period goods (durable goods).

Mono-period Goods and Durable Goods

Mono-period Goods	Durable (poly period) Goods
They are used only once to satisfy a need. They cease to exist once their use was over.	The goods which are used once and the same can be used again in future for several times.
E.g.: foods, productive resources like seeds, fertilizers, etc.	E.g.: land, machinery, implements, tv, mobile, books, etc.

2.4. Desire

It is a social and psychological concept. It is a wish of heart. For e.g. I wish to have a car, big house etc.

2.5. Human Wants

Want refers to a desire, and human wants encompass the limitless desires of individuals. As the saying goes, *"Man is a bundle of desires,"* reflecting the infinite variety and number of human wants. These wants differ from person to person. **Food, shelter, and clothing** constitute the basic necessities of life, essential for survival. However, beyond these necessities, the pursuit shifts towards comfort and enjoyment. As civilization advances, human wants expand—people seek **better food, stylish clothing, comfortable housing, higher education, entertainment,** and numerous other luxuries.

Characteristics of Human wants

1. **Human wants are unlimited**: Human wants are endless. When one desire is fulfilled, another emerges, creating a continuous cycle that never ceases. As a result, human wants constantly multiply, driving an ongoing pursuit of satisfaction.
2. **Any particular want is satiable:** Although wants in aggregate are unlimited, yet it is possible to satisfy a particular want, provided one has the means.
3. **Wants are Complementary:** It is a common experience that our wants often arise in groups. For example, writing a letter requires both paper and a pen—paper alone is insufficient. Similarly, a car needs petrol, oil, and other essentials to function. This interdependence of goods reflects the **complementary nature of wants**.
4. **Wants are competitive:** Our financial resources are limited, yet our desires are numerous. Since we cannot afford everything we want, we must make choices, accepting some desires while forgoing others. This necessity of selection creates **competition among wants**, as we prioritize which to satisfy.

5. **Some wants are both complimentary and competitive:** For example, Factory manager wants machinery and labour. Machinery competes with labour; and up to some extent they also complement each other.
6. **Wants are alternative:** There are several ways of satisfying a particular want. If we feel thirsty, we can have water, soda, sharbat, lassi, thumps-up, Pepsi, etc.
7. **Wants vary with time, place and person:** Wants vary from person to person, and even the same individual desires different things at different times and in different situations.
8. **Wants vary in urgency and intensity:** Some wants are more urgent and intense than others. These pressing needs are typically satisfied first, while less critical ones are either given secondary priority or postponed for later fulfilment.
9. **Wants multiply with civilization:** As civilization spreads among peoples, their wants also go on increasing.
10. **Wants recur:** Most of the human wants are of recurring nature. For example, food, drink, entertainment, etc. We eat something when we feel hungry. It will not last forever. After some hours, we again feel hungry and want some food again and again.
11. **Wants change into habits:** If a particular want is regularly satisfied, a person becomes used to it and it grows into habit. For example, smoking, drug addiction, etc.
12. **Wants are influenced by income, salesmanship and advertisement:** It is obvious that if income is higher, more wants can be satisfied, and a poor man cannot simply afford to have many wants. Besides, we do not always buy the things we need. We often induced to buy particular brands or products by persuasive salesmen or clever advertisement even though better alternatives may be available.
13. **Wants may be the result of custom or convention:** More or less, we all are slaves of custom. Many of our wants are conventional. Whether, we like it or not, we have to spend a lot of money on social ceremonies.

Classification of Wants

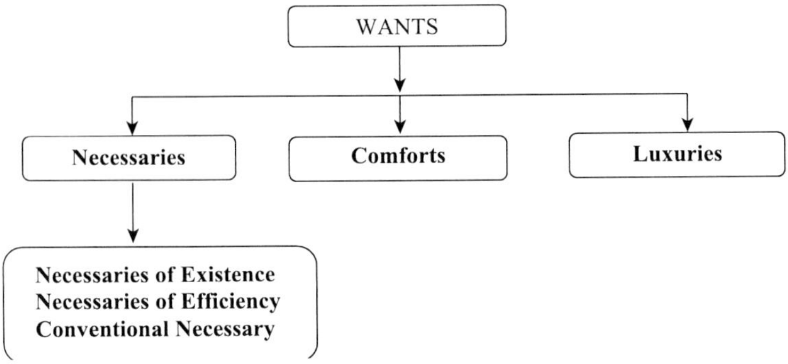

1. Necessaries

They may be sub-divided as:

1. **Necessaries of Existence**: These are the things without which we cannot exist, e.g., food, cloths, shelter, etc.
2. **Necessaries of Efficiency**: Some goods may not be necessary to enable us to live, but necessary to make us efficient workers. A pen is necessary for student.
3. **Conventional Necessary**: These are the things which are forced to use either by social custom or because of the people around us expect us to do so. *Example*: need of black coat for lawyer.

2. Comforts

Having satisfied our wants for the necessaries of life, we desire to have some comforts too. For a student, a book is a necessity, table and a chair are necessaries of efficiency; but cushioned chair is a comfort.

3. Luxuries

Man does not stop even at comforts. After comforts have been provided he wants luxuries too. 'Luxury' has been defined as a superfluous consumption, something we could easily do without. *Example*: costly furniture, luxurious car, etc. For a college student, a fen in summer is a comfort; but air-conditioner is a luxury.

Necessaries, Comforts and Luxuries are relative term

We cannot attach permanent and fixed labels of necessaries, comforts or luxuries to commodities. We cannot say that car is always a luxury. The same thing may be a necessary under one set of conditions and a luxury under others. For example, a car for a doctor is necessary, but for a teacher it is comfort; while for a labour it is luxury. Today what may be a luxury can become a necessary in future. In same manner, what may be regarded as a luxury in India may be a necessary in England. Thus, necessaries, comforts and luxuries are relative to person, time and place.

Comparison / difference

Necessaries of Efficiency	**Comforts**
(1) Necessary to make us efficient workers	(1) Make for fuller life, enjoyments *etc.*
(2) Benefit from money spent is more	(2) Benefit from money spent is less
Comforts	**Luxuries**
(1) Comforts make for a fuller life, enjoyment	(1) It is a superfluous consumption, something we could easily do without it.
(2) Money spent on comforts brings some compensation	(2) Expenditure on luxuries brings negligible return. There may be a loss or harm.

2.6. Utility

Goods serve to satisfy human wants, and this ability is referred to as utility. In simple terms, utility is the capacity of a good to fulfill a human need or desire.

To determine whether a good possesses utility, one must ask: "Does it satisfy a human want?" If the answer is yes, then the good has utility; otherwise, it does not. Both free goods (such as air and water) and economic goods (such as food and clothing) fulfill human wants and, therefore, possess utility.

Utility and Usefulness

A commodity may satisfy a human want, but may not be useful. On contrary, it may actually be injurious e.g., opium, tobacco, poison, etc. But, because they satisfy a human want, we say in Economics that they possess utility, even though their consumption is injurious. The term utility as used in Economics has no ethical or moral significance. Thus, a thing may be good or it may bad, but if it satisfies a human want, we shall say it possesses utility.

Characteristics of Utility

1. **Utility is subjective:** Utility depends on a person's needs and preferences. The same product does not give the same satisfaction to everyone because people have different tastes. For example, a bidi is more useful to a regular smoker than to someone who does not smoke.

Utility varies with purpose

Depending upon the purpose for which a commodity is used, utility of the same varies. Example: Utility derived from water as drinking purpose and irrigation purpose are different.

2. **Utility varies with time:** A particular commodity gives different utilities for the same person in different time period. Cold drinks and ice-cream provide greater utility to the same person in summer than in winter.
3. **Utility varies with ownership:** Ownership of good creates far greater utility from a good than that when it is hired.
4. **Utility need not be synonymous with pleasure:** Utility derived from a commodity is not always linked to **pleasure**. While consuming apples brings enjoyment, consuming medicine may not be pleasurable, even though it has utility. For example, **quinine**, despite its bitter taste, is purchased and consumed because it serves a necessary purpose. Therefore, **utility and pleasure are not the same**—a good may provide utility regardless of whether it brings pleasure or not.
5. **Utility does not mean satisfaction:** Utility is **not the same as satisfaction**; rather, it is the quality of a good that enables it to provide satisfaction to an individual. It would be incorrect to say that a mango **gives utility**; instead, we should say that it **possesses utility** or **provides satisfaction**. A good **has utility**, but it **delivers satisfaction** when consumed.

2.7. Kinds / types / Forms of utility

a) **Form Utility:** By changing the form of a good, great utility can be created. *Examples*: processing of paddy into rice, cotton into cloths, groundnut into oils, etc.

b) **Place Utility:** The utility of a commodity varies based on its geographical location, a concept known as place utility. The process of transporting goods from one region or market to another enhances their utility by making them available where they are scarce. For instance, apples grown in abundance in Himachal Pradesh are transported to the western and southern regions of India, where production is limited, thereby increasing their overall utility and value.

c) **Time Utility:** A time gap between production and consumption gives rise to time utility. By storing commodities over a period, their utility is enhanced, ensuring their availability when demand arises. Thus, storage serves as a vital mechanism in generating time utility.

For instance, agricultural commodities like paddy and wheat are stored to ensure a consistent supply to consumers throughout the year, thereby increasing their utility. Likewise, an umbrella holds greater utility during the rainy season than in winter. This increased usefulness based on timing is referred to as time utility.

d) **Possession Utility:** During the **transaction process**, commodities **change ownership**, passing from one person to another. While commodities have some **utility** in the hands of producers, their **utility increases** when they reach consumers. This increase in utility, resulting from **possession or transfer of ownership**, is known as **possession utility**. For example, the **utility of medicine** is far greater for a **patient** than for the **producer**. Similarly, **milk** holds higher utility for a **child** than for the **milkman** who supplies it.

2.8. Value

Meaning of Value

Value is of two kinds (1) value–in–use and (2) value–in– exchange.

Value-in-use

We often describe education as highly valuable or recognize the great worth of fresh air, sunshine, and rain. In such instances, the term "value" denotes usefulness. This concept, known as value-in-use, is what economists define as utility.

Value-in-exchange

In economics, the term **'value'** is understood as **'value-in-exchange'** rather than mere usefulness. It refers to the **exchangeability** of a good in the market. The **value of a commodity** signifies the quantity of other goods or services that can be obtained in exchange for it. For instance, **fresh air**, despite its immense usefulness, cannot be exchanged for anything, making its **economic value effectively zero**.

Thus, the **value of a commodity** is determined by the goods or services it can command in exchange. In essence, it represents the **purchasing power** of a good in terms of other commodities or services.

Attributes of Value

It is clear, then, that in order to have value in the market; a commodity must not be a free good. Only economic goods can have value in the economic sense. Three qualifications are thus essential for a good before it can have value:

1. It must possess utility;
2. It must be scare in relation to demand; and
3. It must be transferable or marketable.

All three qualities—utility, scarcity, and transferability—must coexist for a good to have value. In the absence of any one of these qualities, a good holds no economic value. For instance, air has utility but is not scarce, while rotten eggs may be scarce but lack utility. Conversely, a book possesses utility, is scarce, and is transferable. Therefore, in economic terms, air and rotten eggs hold no value, whereas a book has value.

Value is relative term

Since 'value' in Economics means value-in-exchange, it must be relative. It cannot be absolute. It is impossible to speak of the value of a commodity in an absolute manner independently of anything else.

For example, to say that the value of a book is great, gives an idea of its utility only. To talk of the value of a book, in economic sense, we must relate it to something else which we can get in exchange for it. Say, value of a book is Rs. 100 or say value of a book is equal to value of 5 kg rice.

Value equates certain commodities, i.e., a book may fetch 5 kg of rice. It expresses relationship between two commodities, it relates one to other. That is why value is said to be relative. If value of a book increase, it may fetch >5 kg of rice; while if value of rice increases, a book may fetch <5 kg of rice.

2.9. Money

It refers to anything which is generally accepted as a medium of exchange.

2.10. Price

Value and price are distinct concepts. When value is measured in monetary terms, it is referred to as price.

In prehistoric times, before the advent of money, people exchanged goods directly for other goods—a system known as barter. However, in the modern economy, goods and services are typically exchanged for money. Consequently, the price of a commodity today represents its monetary value. In essence, price is the expression of value in terms of money.

Economists generally do not differentiate between **value and price**, as all **prices** are interconnected, forming a **price system**. This system plays a **crucial role in a capitalist economy**, where buyers convey their demand for goods

through prices. Every price paid for a commodity acts as a **vote in its favor**, influencing production and allocation. Ultimately, it is the **price system** that governs the **economic activities** of a society.

2.11. Wealth

In everyday language, **wealth** is often associated with **money or riches**. However, in **economics**, the term has a **broader** and more **specific meaning**. It refers to **scarce goods** that satisfy **human wants** and possess **monetary value**. Any item that holds **money value** is considered **wealth**. Since all **economic goods** have **value-in-exchange**, wealth encompasses all such goods. In economics, the term **wealth** is synonymous with **economic goods**. It is defined as the **"stock of goods existing at a given time that have monetary value."** Thus, in economic terms, even the **poorest individual** possesses some **wealth**.

Attributes of Wealth or Characteristics of Wealth

There are three attributes of wealth as in the case of value; Utility, Scarcity and Transferability or Marketability. Three qualifications are thus essential for a good before it can be considered as wealth:

1. **It must possess utility:** It must have the power to satisfy a want.
2. **It must be scare**: For example, **air and sunshine** are essential for life. We cannot live without them. But we do not consider them as wealth because they are available in large quantities. Such goods are known as free goods. The goods which are scare are wealth.
3. **It must be transferable:** That is, it should be possible for us to transfer the ownership from one person to another. Land, buildings, machinery, etc. are examples of wealth. **Degree certificate**, skill of doctor, artists, cricket, etc. is non-transferable; hence they are not considered as wealth though they are source of wealth. But the **goodwill** of a company is transferable; hence, it is a wealth.

Classification of wealth

Wealth can be classified as follows:

(1) **Individual wealth:** The wealth of an individual consists of his property like cash, land, buildings, livestock and goodwill of business which commands a price in the market.

(2) **Personal wealth:** Personal qualities like skill, ability and intelligence.

(3) **Social or communal wealth:** It consists of state, municipal or social properties like dams, canals, state and museums.

(4) **National wealth:** Narrowly speaking it consists of the aggregate wealth of all citizens, excluding the debts. In the wider sense, it includes rivers, mountains, high character of people *etc.*

(5) **Cosmopolitan wealth:** It is the wealth of the whole world.

(6) **Negative wealth:** This refers to debts owned by individuals or state. If something is a nuisance like wild pigs, or stray cattles damaging the crops, it may be regarded as negative wealth.

(7) **Representative wealth:** Documents of title, documents of property, insurance policy *etc* are representative wealth.

2.12. Welfare

Welfare is the well-being of individual or community. It refers to the condition of mind. Hence, any good whether it is free or economic, is counted as long as it leads to welfare. Hence, **Welfare = Wealth (all economic goods) + All Free goods.**

Wealth and Welfare are two different aspects having relationship. All economics goods are wealth. Free goods have no place while representing wealth. Wealth is a path for welfare, as all our desires are satisfied by means of wealth.

2.13. Capital

In the ordinary language, capital is used in the sense of money. But when we talk of capital as a factor of production, it is quite wrong to confuse capital with money. There is no doubt that money is a form of wealth and it yields income when it is lent out. But it cannot be called capital. Capital is a factor of production, but money as such does not serve as a factor of production. It is another thing that with money we can buy machinery and raw materials which then serve as factors of production. Capital refers to wealth in the form of money or assets, taken as a sign of the financial strength of an individual, organization or nation and assumed to be available for development or investment. So, capital has been defined as that parts of a person's wealth other than land which yields an income or which aids in the production of further wealth.

- Capital is a factor of production that is used to create goods or service.
- Capital is defined as any financial resources or assets owned by a business that are useful in furthering development and generating income.
- According to Karl Marx, "capital is *crystallized labour*" This is indicated in his book, 'Das Kapital'.

2.14. Income

In economics, when we refer to income, generally we mean money income. We know that all economic goods form wealth. The main source of income is wealth. For example, if you own a house, it is your wealth. If you get rent from it, it is your income.

- **According to Seligman,** "Income in the economic sense is the flow of satisfactions from economic goods".
- It is defined as the flow of cash or cash-equivalents received from work (wage or salary), capital (interest or profit), or land (rent).
- It is defined as money or other forms of payment (received periodically or regularly) from commerce, employment, endowment, investment, royalties etc.
- It is defined as money earned from working that requires your time. You actively work and you are paid for it.

Classification of Income

There are followings kinds of income

- **Money income:** Generally people earn their incomes in the form of money. Money income is also known as nominal income.
- **Real income:** Real income refers to the income of an individual or group after taking into consideration the effects of inflation on purchasing power. For example, if you receive a 2% salary increase over the previous year and inflation for the year is 1%, then your real income only increases by 1%. Conversely, if you receive a 2% raise in salary and inflation is at 3%, then your real income shrinks by 1%. As real income measures the purchasing power of an individual's wages, analysts often compare it to the Consumer Price Index (CPI).So, Real income is price adjusted money income.
- **Earned (Active) Income:** Money earned from working that requires your time. You actively work, and you are paid for it. Examples: Salary; wages; bonuses; contract work.
- **Portfolio Income:** Money from selling an investment for more than what you paid. Examples: Stocks, bonds, mutual funds, interest, etc.; money from buying/selling real estate or other assets, such as automobiles.
- **Passive Income:** Money generated from assets you own, where you are not actively working. Examples: Rental income, business income.
- **National Income:** National income refers to the value of commodities and services produced by a country during a year.

- **Per capita Income:** We get per capita income by dividing national income by the population of the country.

$$Per\ capita\ income = \frac{National\ Income}{Population}$$

Difference between income and wealth

Income	**Wealth**
Income is earned or received during a limited period	Wealth is accumulated over time.
Income is flow of money obtained from factor of production.	Wealth is a market price of the stock of asset possessed by individual or household
e.g. A person investing 2 lakh, he earns Rs. 10,000 as interest. This is his income	*e.g.* A person is having Rs. 2 lakhs *i.e.* wealth.

3

Agricultural Economics

3.1. Agriculture

- The term agriculture originates from the Latin words *ager*, meaning soil, and *cultura,* meaning cultivation.
- In its broadest sense, agriculture refers to the cultivation of crops and the rearing of livestock for production.
- It is essentially synonymous with farming, involving the field-based production of food, fodder, and industrial organic materials.

3.2. Economics

- Economics is the science that studies as how people choose to use scare productive resources (like land, labour, capital and organiser) to produce various goods and to distribute these goods to various members of the society for their consumption.

3.3. Agricultural Economics

- Agricultural economics is a branch of applied economics that applies the principles of choice to the efficient use of scarce resources such as land, labor, water, seeds, and fertilizers in farming and related activities.
- It focuses on guiding farmers in the optimal utilization of land, labor, and capital.
- Its significance lies in providing practical solutions to help farmers maximize income while managing limited resources effectively.

3.4. Definitions

1. Prof. Gray has defined agricultural economics as ***"The science in which the principles and methods of economics are applied to the special conditions of agricultural industry"***.
2. According to Prof. Hibbard ***"Agricultural economics is the study of relationships arising from the wealth-getting and wealth-using activity of man in agriculture".***

Thus, agricultural economics deals with the problems of the farms as the units of industry, the income earning and spending activities of the farmers and also the management of farm business and bringing necessary changes according to the situation so as to bring stability to farm income.

3.5. Characteristics of agriculture

Agriculture is a critical sector of the economy and plays a vital role in providing food, fibre, and various raw materials. It is characterized by several key features, which include:

- **Biological Production**: Agriculture involves the cultivation of crops and the raising of livestock, which are biological processes. It relies on the growth and development of plants and animals, making it subject to the challenges of weather, pests, and diseases.
- **Seasonal Nature**: Agricultural activities are often seasonal, with planting and harvesting times determined by factors like climate and the life cycles of crops and animals. This seasonality can lead to fluctuating workloads for farmers.
- **Land-Based**: Agriculture relies on the use of land as a primary resource. The quality and availability of arable land significantly impact agricultural productivity. Different types of agriculture, such as crop farming, animal husbandry, and horticulture, use land in various ways.
- **Labour-Intensive**: Many agricultural tasks require manual labour, such as planting, weeding, harvesting, and tending to animals. Labour-intensive practices can be prevalent, especially in traditional or small-scale farming.
- **Capital-Intensive**: Modern agriculture also requires substantial capital investment in machinery, equipment, and technology. Large-scale farming operations often use advanced machinery to increase productivity.
- **Risk and Uncertainty**: Agriculture is susceptible to various risks, including weather-related risks (droughts, floods, frost), pest and disease outbreaks, technological, market price fluctuations, institutional etc. These factors can lead to uncertainty for farmers.
- **Environmental Impact**: Agriculture has significant environmental implications. It can affect soil quality, water resources and biodiversity. Sustainable farming practices aim to minimize negative environmental impacts.

- **Global Trade**: Agriculture is a global industry, with many countries producing and trading agricultural goods. International trade in agricultural products is common, and it plays a crucial role in global food security and economic development.
- **Technological Advances**: Modern agriculture has seen substantial technological advancements, including the use of genetically modified crops, precision agriculture, and automation in farming processes. These innovations have increased productivity and efficiency.
- **Diversity of Practices**: It encompasses a wide range of practices, including subsistence farming, commercial farming, organic farming, agribusiness, and more. Practices can vary significantly by region and culture.
- **Food Production**: One of the primary purposes of agriculture is food production. It provides the majority of the world's food supply, including cereals, fruits, vegetables, meat, dairy, and other essential food items.
- **Cultural and Social Significance**: Agriculture is often deeply intertwined with the culture and social fabric of communities. It can shape traditions, rituals, and social structures.
- **Government Involvement**: Many governments have policies and regulations related to agriculture, including subsidies, price supports, land-use planning, and environmental regulations. Government involvement can significantly influence the agricultural sector.

3.6. Challenges and Opportunities

Agriculture faces various challenges, including the need to increase production to meet the demands of a growing global population, address environmental sustainability and adapt to changing climate conditions. However, it also presents opportunities for innovation, income generation and rural development.

3.7. Importance and its role in economic development

Agriculture plays a pivotal role in economic development and holds significant importance in various ways:

- **Food Security**: Agriculture is the primary source of food production. It ensures a stable and sufficient food supply, which is essential for the well-being of a nation's population. Food and nutritional security is a fundamental requirement for economic development, as hungry or malnourished populations are less productive and face health challenges.

- **Income Generation**: Agriculture provides livelihoods for a substantial portion of the world's population. In many developing countries, a significant percentage of the labour force is engaged in agriculture. It serves as a source of income and employment, especially in rural areas.
- **Poverty Reduction**: Agriculture can be a powerful tool for poverty reduction. When properly managed and supported, it can generate income for small-scale farmers and improve their living standards. Reducing poverty is a crucial component of economic development.
- **Rural Development**: Agriculture is often the economic backbone of rural communities. Investments in agriculture can stimulate rural development by creating jobs, improving infrastructure, and boosting local economies.
- **Raw Materials and Exports**: Agriculture provides raw materials for various industries, including textiles, agro-processing, and bio-fuels. Agricultural exports can contribute significantly to a nation's foreign exchange earnings, promoting economic growth.
- **Market for Non-Agricultural Goods**: A thriving agricultural sector can create a market for non-agricultural goods and services. As farmers' incomes rise, they have the capacity to purchase products and services from other sectors, leading to economic diversification.
- **Innovation and Technology**: Agriculture has seen technological advancements that have improved productivity, such as the use of modern machinery, genetically modified crops, and precision agriculture. These innovations can have spillover effects on other sectors of the economy.
- **Environmental Sustainability**: Sustainable agriculture practices are essential for protecting the environment and ensuring long-term economic development. Sustainable agriculture aims to minimize the negative impact on ecosystems, soil, and water resources.
- **Rural-Urban Linkages**: Agriculture can strengthen the linkages between rural and urban areas. The flow of agricultural products to urban centres and the influx of agricultural inputs from urban areas create synergies and promote economic interdependence.
- **Infrastructure Development**: Investment in agriculture often requires the development of essential infrastructure, such as roads, storage facilities, and irrigation systems. This infrastructure benefits not only the agricultural sector but also the broader economy.
- **Resilience to Shocks**: A diversified agricultural sector can enhance a nation's resilience to economic shocks and crises. It provides a buffer against price volatility and supply disruptions in global markets.

- **Economic Growth**: Agriculture contributes to economic growth by increasing overall production and income. A vibrant agricultural sector can stimulate growth in related industries and support overall economic development.
- **Trade Opportunities**: Agricultural products are often traded internationally, providing opportunities for export earnings and trade relationships. Access to global markets can enhance economic development.
- **Human Capital Development**: Agriculture can support human capital development by providing education and skills training in rural areas. An educated and skilled workforce is essential for economic progress.
- **Economic Transformation**: In many developing countries, agriculture is a stepping stone for broader economic transformation. As agriculture becomes more productive and efficient, surplus labour is freed up for other sectors, promoting industrialization and services.

3.8. Scope of agricultural economics

It analysis the micro as well macro nits of production. Agricultural economics is helpful in studies of input and output interrelationship, marketing of input as well output to increase the income and level of satisfaction. It also includes the national, international problems of agricultural system and also considers the social welfare of the farming community. The subject matter of agricultural economics is divided into production, consumption, exchange, distribution and public finance.

3.9. Division of agricultural economics

Agricultural economics is mainly divided into following subjects:

- **Production economics**: it is mainly concerned with the allocation of scarce recourses among the production activities of the economy
- **Farm management**: Farm management as carried out by farmers has been defined (Dillon 1980, p. 258) as 'the process by which resources and situations are manipulated by the farm manager in trying, with less than full information, to achieve his [or her] goals'.
- **Agricultural marketing:** Marketing is the activity of identifying and satisfying need and wants of customers in profitable way Agricultural Marketing is the study of all the activities, agencies, and polices involved in the procurement of farm inputs by the farmers and the movement of agricultural products from the farm to the consumers.

- **Agricultural finance**: Agricultural finance encompasses a range of financial services designed to support both on-farm and off-farm agricultural activities and enterprises. It includes funding for input supply, production, distribution, wholesale, processing, and marketing.
- **Labour economics**: In economics, labor refers to the effort exerted by human beings in the production process. It is traditionally distinguished from other factors of production, such as land and capital. Some economic theories introduce the concept of human capital, which emphasizes the skills and knowledge workers possess rather than just their physical labor.
- **Rural economics**: Rural economics is the study of rural economies, including: farm and non-farm industry. Economic growth, development, and change. Size and spatial distribution of production and household units and interregional trade.
- **Micro and Macro-economics**: Microeconomics focuses on specific markets and segments of the economy, examining aspects such as consumer behavior, individual labor markets, and the theory of firms. In contrast, macroeconomics analyzes the economy as a whole, addressing broader economic factors and trends.

4

Agricultural Planning and Development in the Country

4.1. Introduction

The agricultural sector plays a vital role in a nation's economic development. It has been a key driver of prosperity in advanced economies and remains essential for the progress of developing nations. In regions with low per capita real income, agriculture and other primary industries are given high priority. As Dr. Bright Singh emphasizes, *"An increase in agricultural production, along with a rise in the per capita income of the rural population, fosters industrialization and urbanization, thereby boosting demand for industrial goods."*

The historical trajectory of England provides clear evidence that the Agricultural Revolution preceded and laid the foundation for the Industrial Revolution. Similarly, in the United States and Japan, agricultural advancement has played a pivotal role in fostering industrialization. Many developing nations, in their pursuit of economic growth, have recognized the limitations of an excessive focus on industrialization as a sole strategy for achieving higher per capita real income.

Industrial and agricultural development are not substitutes but rather complementary forces that mutually reinforce each other in terms of both inputs and outputs. Empirical observations indicate that enhanced agricultural productivity and output significantly contribute to a nation's overall economic progress. Therefore, prioritizing the further development of the agricultural sector is both rational and essential.

As Dr. Bright Singh emphasizes, "An increase in agricultural production, along with a rise in the per capita income of the rural community, coupled with industrialization and urbanization, leads to heightened demand for industrial goods." In this manner, the agricultural sector serves as a catalyst for economic growth by supporting and supplementing industrial expansion.

Muir further elaborates on this synergy, stating, "Agricultural progress is crucial for supplying food to the expanding non-agricultural labor force, providing raw materials for industry, generating savings and tax revenues to finance broader economic development, earning foreign exchange, and fostering a growing market for domestic manufacturing."."

According to Prof. Kinderberger, Todaro, Lewis and Nurkse etc., agriculture makes its contribution to economic development in several ways viz:

- Supplying food and raw materials to non-agricultural sectors of the economy.
- Generating demand for goods produced in non-agricultural sectors, as rural populations utilize their purchasing power derived from selling marketable surpluses.
- Contributing investable surpluses in the form of savings and tax revenues, which can be allocated to non-agricultural development.
- Earning valuable foreign exchange through the export of agricultural commodities.
- Providing employment opportunities to a large segment of uneducated, underprivileged, and unskilled labor.

4.2. Role of Agriculture in Economic Development

The agricultural sector serves as the backbone of an economy, supplying essential resources for human sustenance and raw materials for industrialization. Its significance in economic development can be outlined as follows:

- **Contribution to National Income:** The economic history of many advanced nations demonstrates that agricultural prosperity has played a crucial role in driving economic progress. It is rightly observed that "The world's leading industrialized nations were once primarily agrarian, whereas developing economies still rely heavily on agriculture, which remains a significant contributor to national income." In India, agriculture continues to account for 28% of the national income.
- **Source of Food Supply:** Agriculture serves as the fundamental source of food for all nations, regardless of their level of development. In underdeveloped and developing countries, rapid population growth has led to an escalating demand for food. If the agricultural sector fails to meet this rising demand, it can hinder overall economic growth. Thus, increasing food production is essential for sustaining economic development. The demand for food within an economy is determined by the following equation:

D-P+2g

Here,

D stands for Annual Rate of Growth in demand for food.

P stands for Population Growth Rate.

g stands for Rate of Increase in per Capita Income.

2 stand for Income Elasticity of Demand for Agricultural Products.

- **Pre-Requisite for Raw Material:** Agricultural advancement is essential for ensuring a steady supply of raw materials to agro-based industries, particularly in developing countries. A shortage of agricultural commodities directly affects industrial production, leading to a rise in the general price level and hindering overall economic growth. Numerous industries, including flour mills, rice shellers, oil and dal mills, sugar factories, meat and dairy processing units, bakeries, wineries, jute mills, and textile mills, rely heavily on agricultural output for their operations.
- **Provision of Surplus:** Advancements in agriculture lead to surplus production, enabling the growth of agricultural exports. In the early stages of economic development, increasing export earnings is especially vital, as it helps ease the strain on foreign exchange reserves required for importing essential capital goods. Johnson and Mellor highlight this perspective, stating, *"Considering the pressing need for higher foreign exchange earnings and the limited availability of alternative opportunities, expanding agricultural exports is often a prudent strategy, even when global supply-demand conditions for a commodity seem unfavorable".*
- **Shift of Manpower:** In the early stages of economic development, agriculture serves as the primary employer, absorbing a significant portion of the labor force. In India, approximately 62% of the workforce remains engaged in this sector. Agricultural progress enables the gradual transition of labor from agriculture to non-agricultural sectors, which is essential for economic growth. This shift is particularly important as it alleviates the pressure of surplus labor on limited land resources. Therefore, the release of excess manpower from agriculture is not only crucial for enhancing agricultural productivity but also for facilitating the expansion of non-agricultural industries.
- **Creation of Infrastructure:** Agricultural development necessitates the establishment of essential infrastructure such as roads, market yards, storage facilities, transportation networks, railways, and postal services. This, in turn, generates demand for industrial products and fosters the growth of the commercial sector.

- **Relief from Shortage of Capital:** The advancement of the agricultural sector has alleviated the financial strain on several developed countries that previously faced shortages of foreign capital. Reliance on foreign capital often comes with restrictive conditions, creating additional economic challenges. However, since agricultural development requires relatively lower capital investment, it reduces dependency on foreign funds and mitigates associated growth constraints.
- **Helpful to Reduce Inequality:** In an agrarian and densely populated country, income inequality between rural and urban areas tends to be significant. To address this disparity, prioritizing agricultural development is essential. Enhancing agricultural prosperity can elevate the income of the rural population, thereby helping to narrow the income gap to some extent.
- **Based on Democratic Notions:** If the agricultural sector fails to grow at a sufficient pace, it can lead to widespread discontent among the population, posing a threat to the stability of democratic governance. Economic development requires the mitigation of both political and social tensions, which can be effectively achieved through agricultural progress. By fostering growth in this sector, the majority of the population can be given tangible hopes for prosperity, thereby ensuring social harmony and political stability. Thus, agricultural development is not only an economic necessity but also a crucial factor in maintaining political and social equilibrium.
- **Create Effective Demand:** The development of the agricultural sector enhances the purchasing power of farmers, thereby driving growth in the non-agricultural sector by creating a larger market for increased production. In underdeveloped countries, where the majority of the population relies on agriculture, their ability to afford and consume manufactured goods is crucial for overall economic expansion. Additionally, higher productivity in cash crops can facilitate the transition to a more exchange-oriented economy, further stimulating non-agricultural growth. Moreover, increased demand for industrial products such as pesticides, farm machinery, and other agricultural inputs provides a significant boost to industrial output.
- **Helpful in Phasing out Economic Depression:** During periods of economic depression, industrial production can be curtailed or halted, but agricultural production persists as it supplies essential necessities for survival. Consequently, the agricultural sector continues to generate effective demand, even amid unfavorable economic conditions, ensuring a degree of stability within the economy.

- **Source of Foreign Exchange for the Country:** In many developing countries, primary products constitute a significant portion—ranging from 60 to 70 percent—of total export earnings. Consequently, the ability to import capital goods and machinery essential for industrial development is heavily dependent on agricultural export revenues. If agricultural exports fail to grow at a sufficiently rapid pace, these nations may face large deficits in their balance of payments, leading to severe foreign exchange constraints. However, primary commodities often experience declining prices in the international market, limiting their potential to generate sustained export earnings. Recognizing this challenge, large developing nations like India, which possess strong industrial growth potential, are actively working to diversify their production structures. To enhance their export portfolios, they are promoting the sale of manufactured goods, even if this initially necessitates protective trade policies during the early phases of economic planning.
- **Contribution to Capital Formation:** Underdeveloped and developing countries require substantial capital for economic development. In the early stages of growth, agriculture serves as a vital source of capital formation. The agricultural sector contributes to capital accumulation through various mechanisms, including:
  (i) **Agricultural taxation** – Generating revenue for public investment.
  (ii) **Export of agricultural products** – Earning foreign exchange to finance development.
  (iii) **Government price policies** – Procuring agricultural goods at lower prices and selling them at higher rates, a strategy historically employed by Russia and China.
  (iv) **Utilization of disguised unemployment** – Excess labor in agriculture is considered a potential source of investible surplus.
  (v) **Reallocation of resources** – Shifting labor and capital from agriculture to non-farm sectors to promote industrialization and economic diversification.
- **Employment Opportunities for Rural People:** Agriculture serves as a major source of employment for rural populations in underdeveloped and developing countries, playing a vital role in sustaining livelihoods. In addition to agricultural activities, landless laborers and marginal farmers often engage in non-agricultural occupations such as handicrafts, furniture-making, textiles, leatherwork, metal industries, processing units, and various service sectors. These rural enterprises primarily cater to local market demands. In India, approximately 70.6% of the

total labor force remains dependent on agriculture for their livelihood, highlighting the sector's critical role in employment generation.

- **Improving Rural Welfare:** In an underdeveloped country, the rural economy primarily relies on agriculture and allied activities. The growth of agricultural surplus, driven by increased production and productivity, significantly enhances social welfare, particularly in rural areas. As agricultural prosperity rises, the living standards of rural communities improve, enabling them to afford a more nutritious diet that includes eggs, milk, ghee, and fruits. Additionally, higher incomes allow them to enjoy a more comfortable lifestyle with modern amenities such as better housing, motorcycles, radios, televisions, and improved clothing, fostering overall rural development.
- **Extension of Market for Industrial Output:** Agricultural progress directly contributes to the expansion of markets for industrial goods. Increased agricultural productivity enhances the income levels of the rural population, which, in turn, stimulates greater demand for industrial products, thereby fostering the growth of the industrial sector. Thus, agricultural development serves as a fundamental driver of overall economic progress. Even in developed nations, significant emphasis is placed on advancing agriculture, recognizing its crucial role in sustaining economic growth and stability.

5

Demand

5.1. Meaning

Demand in economics means a desire to possess a good supported by willingness and ability to pay for it. If you have a desire to buy a tractor, but do not have the adequate means to pay for it, it will simply be a wish, a desire or a want and not demand. Demand is an effective desire, i.e., a desire which is backed by willingness and ability to pay for a commodity in order to obtain it. In the words, "*Demand means the various quantities of a good that consumer willing and able to purchase at various price during a particular period of time in a given place/market*". Thus, demand in economics implies both the desire to purchase and the ability to pay for a good.

5.2. Definitions

1. **According to Prof. J M Keynes,** "emphasized the importance of effective demand, which is the total amount of goods and services that consumers are willing and able to purchase at various price levels, taking into account their income and other factors".
2. **According to Alfred Marshall,** "the amount demanded of a commodity is the amount that buyers are able and willing to purchase at a given price in a given time period."
3. **According to John Maynard Keynes:** "demand as the total amount of goods and services that individuals, businesses and the government are willing and able to purchase at various price levels".
4. **According to Milton Friedman** "demand as the quantity of a good or service that people are willing to buy at a specific price, influenced by their utility and income".
5. **According to Paul Samuelson** "demand as the quantity of a product that consumers are willing to buy at different prices, holding other factors constant".
6. **According to Joan Robinson** "demand is effective only when it leads to actual purchases and it depends not only on individual preferences

and prices but also on the state of the economy, including employment and income levels".

7. **According to Leon Walras** "demand as the set of consumer preferences and budget constraints that determine the quantities of goods and services consumers will purchase at given prices".
8. **According to Prof. Mayer says** "The demand for a good is a schedule of the amount that the buyers would be willing to purchase at all possible prices at any time".

Therefore, we can say that demand is a effective desire of a commodity which is expressed with reference to a particular time and a particular price.

Elements of demand: the essential elements of demand are

- There must be a desire for a particular commodity
- Desired commodity must be available in the market
- The consumer must have sufficient money to purchase the commodity
- The consumer must be ready to spare the money for the purchase of commodity
- The demand must be expressed at a particular price
- The demand must be expressed with reference to a particular time.

5.3. Law of demand

Law of demand explains the relationship between price and demand of a commodity. Demand of a commodity decreases if its price increases and the demand increases it its price falls, other things being remains constant. Thus, the law of demand explains inverse relationship between price and quantity demanded (Figure 5.3).

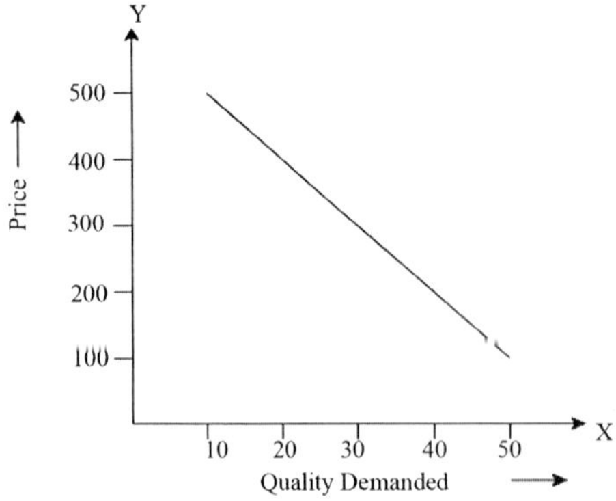

Law of Demand

- **According to Prof. A Marshall** "the greater the amount to be sold, the smaller must be the price at which it is offered in order that it may find purchasers; in other words, the amount demanded increases with a fall in price and diminishes with a rise in prices".
- **According to Prof. PA Samuelson** "when the price of a goods is raised (at the same time that of all other things are held constant) less of it will be demanded, people will buy more at lower price and buy less at higher prices".

5.3.1. Assumptions of law of demand

"Other things remain constant" is an important phrase of the law of demand. This clause explains assumptions of on which it is based. These assumption are the conditions that should be fulfilled for the application of this law. According to Prof. Mayers, the assumptions of the law are as under:

- Income of the consumer remain constant.
- There should be no change in the habits or tastes of consumers.
- There should be no change in the price of the related commodity.
- No new substitute of the commodity should be developed.

5.3.2. Causes of the application of law of demand or reason for downward sloping demand curve

- **Law of diminishing marginal utility:** law of demand is based upon the law of diminishing marginal utility. This law states that as a consumer increases the consumption of all other commodities, consumption of every additional unit of the commodity provides him declining utility. Due to this reason, consumer will purchase additional unit of a commodity when he gets it at a lower price. For this reason, demand at higher prices is less and at lower prices is more.
- **Substitution effect**: substitution effect is an important cause of the application of law of demand. When the price of a commodity increases, consumers prefer to purchase its substitute goods because they falls, consumers prefer to consume this commodity in place of its substitute goods.
- **Income effect**: decrease in price of a commodity is equal to an increase in the income of the individual. Because now they will have to spend less to purchase the same quantity of commodity as earlier. Similarly increase in price of a commodity is equal to decrease in the income of consumers and will result in decrease in the demand of commodity.

5.3.3. Changes in the number of consumers

Suppose the price of a commodity changes (either increase or decrease), it will affect its demand in following ways.

1. Many consumer changes over to its substitutes
2. Consumers who continue to use this commodity, will change the quantity of their consumption.

As a result of these effects, demand of the commodity will change.

5.3.4. Diverse uses of a commodity

If a commodity can be put to a number of uses, its demand will be greatly affected by a change in its price. Example, In case of electricity price increases very high, its use may be restricted only to essential uses and if its prices decreases, it can be used for all the uses.

5.3.5. Exception to the law of demand

1. **Giffen's paradox**: Sir Robert Giffen discovered that the poor people will demand more of inferior goods if their prices rise and demand less if their prices fall. Inferior goods are those goods which people buy in large quantities when they are poor and in small quantities when they become rich. For example, poor people spend the major part of their income on coarse grains (e.g. ragi, kodra, bavta) and only a small part on rice. When the price of coarse grains rises, they will buy less rice. To fill up the resulting gap, more of coarse grains have to be purchased. Thus, rise in the price of coarse grains results in the increase in quantity of coarse grains purchased. This is called 'Giffen Paradox'. In these cases, the law of demand has an exception.
2. **Veblen Goods/ Conspicuous (prominent): I**t observed that certain goods are sought after by the wealthy as a symbol of social prestige. For such goods, a rise in price enhances their exclusivity, making them more desirable and leading to increased demand. For instance, higher diamond prices may drive greater demand among the affluent. If these goods were inexpensive, they would lose their appeal, and the wealthy might not purchase them at all.
3. **High priced commodities:** this law does not apply on high priced commodities also because the consumers purchase these commodities due to their high price such as cream, powder, other items of cosmetics and decorative pieces etc.

4. **Emergencies:** law of demand does not apply in case of emergencies such as war, famine, curfew etc. Under such emergencies, the price of most of the commodities increase but still their demand increases.
5. **Ignorance of consumers**: Prof. Benham stated that ignorance of consumers is also a factor that induces them to purchase more of a commodity at a higher price. Some are the consumers who feel that high priced goods are better than low priced one.

5.4. Demand schedule

Law of demand can be illustrated with the help of a demand schedule and demand curve. Demand schedule is the schedule which expresses different quantities of a commodity demanded at its different prices. Demand schedule is of two type:

5.4.1. Individual demand schedule

It is a demanding schedule that depicts the demand of an individual customer for a commodity in relation to its price. Let us study it with the help of an example.

Table 5.4.1: Individual Demand schedule

Price (Rs./unit)	Qty Demanded (units)
1	100
2	80
3	65
4	55
5	47
6	40
7	34
8	29
9	25
10	22

The above schedule depicts the individual demand schedule. We can see that when the price of the commodity is INR 100, its demand is 50 units. Similarly, when its price is INR 500, its demand decreases to 10 units.

Individual Demand Curve

It is a graphical representation of the individual demand schedule. The X-axis represents the demand and Y-axis represents the price of a commodity.

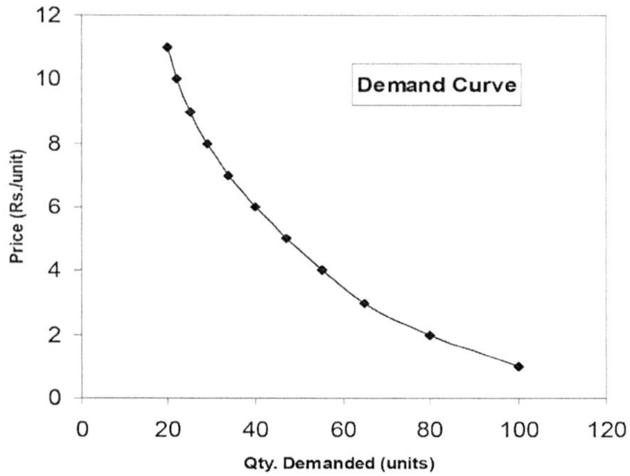

Individual Demand Curve

The demand curve is often illustrated as a straight line, implying a linear relationship between price and demand. However, in reality, demand curves tend to be non-linear. No business can precisely determine the exact shape of a product's demand curve. Instead, they rely on real-time market data to assess demand conditions. Over time, businesses accumulate market insights, allowing them to refine their understanding of demand-price dynamics and gain a strategic advantage in pricing and production decisions.

Thus, we can conclude that as the price falls the demand increases and as the price raises the demand decreases. Hence, there exists an inverse relationship between the price and quantity demanded.

5.4.2. Market demand schedule

Market demand schedule expresses different quantities of a commodity that can be sold in a market at its different prices. A market demand schedule is an aggregate of individual demand schedule of all the individual consumers of a commodity in a market. Following is an imaginary market demand schedule of a commodity.

Table 5.4.2: Market Demand Schedule for Apple

Price (Rs. Per Kg.)	Individual demand schedule (Rs./ Kg.)		Market demand (A+B)
	Buyer A	Buyer B	
10	1	0	1
09	3	1	4
08	7	2	9
07	11	4	15
06	13	6	19

The above schedule shows the market demand for apple. When the price of the apple is ₹10, customer A demands 1 units while the customer B demands 0 units.

Thus, the market demand is 1 units. Similarly, when its price is ₹ 6, Customer A demands 13 units while customer B demands 6 units. Thus, it's market demand increase to 19 units.

Market Demand Curve

It is a graphical representation of the market demand schedule. The X-axis represents the demand and Y-axis represents the price of a commodity. The Particular in table are graphically depicted to represent the demand curve of consumer A and B and the entire market (Figure 5.3). The market demand curve for apple is drawn based on the first and last columns of the table.

Market demand Schedule

5.5. Shift in demand curve or movement along demand curve

5.5.1. Increase and Decrease in Demand or shift in demand curve

- Lead to shift in demand curve
- Caused by factor other than price of that commodity.
- Increase in demand means more demand at same price or the same demand at higher price.
- Decrease in demand means less demand at the same price or the same demand at lower prices.

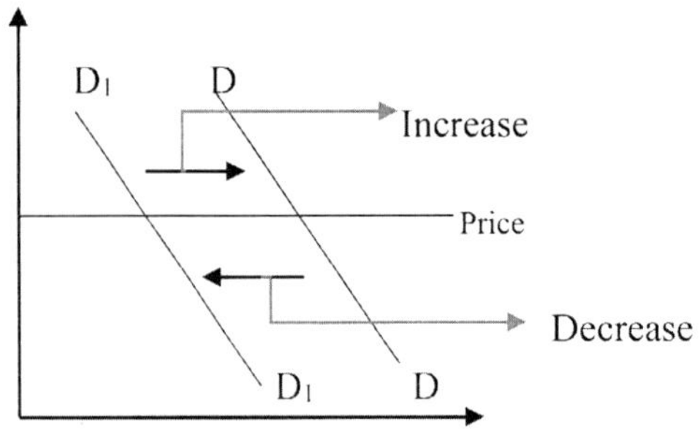

5.5.2. Extension and Contraction in Demand or Movement along demand curve

- Lead to movement in the demand curve.
- Caused due to change in price.
- Extension in demand means an increase in quantity demand due to decrease in prices of the commodity under consideration (keeping all other factor are constant).

Contraction in demand means decease in quantity demand due to increase in prices of the commodity under consideration (keeping all other factor are constant).

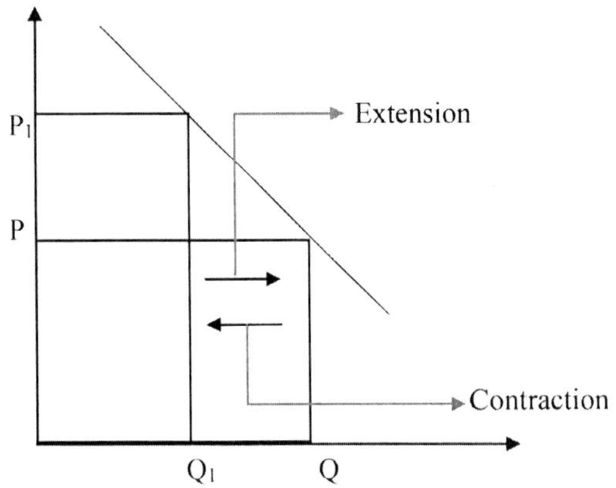

5.5.3. Type of Demand: various types of demand can be explained as given under

1. **Price Demand:** It refers to the various quantities of a commodity or service that a consumer would purchase at a given time in a market at various hypothetical prices if other things remain the same.

2. **Income Demand:** It refers to various quantities of goods or services that a consumer is willing to purchase at different level of income ceteris paribus.
3. **Cross Demand:** The cross demand means the quantities of a goods or services which will be purchased by a consumer with references to the change in the price of substitution goods. Example Tea and Coffee.
4. **Autonomous Demand:** The goods whose demand is not linked with the demand of the other goods are supposed to have autonomous demand.
5. **Derived Demand:** The demand for the certain goods related with the demand for other goods are called derived demand. Example, demand of seed, fertilizer and chemical is the derived demand because for agricultural product.
6. **Inferior goods**: there is inverse relationship between the demand of inferior goods and income of consumers. Demand of inferior goods decreases on an increase in the income of consumers and increases on a fall in the income of consumers.
7. **Complementary goods**: complementary goods are those that are used with a particular goods such as pen and ink, bike and petrol, bread and butter etc. when the price of a commodity increases, demand of its complementary goods will decrease along with the demand of original goods. For example if the price of car increases not only demand of car will decrease but the demand of petrol will also decreases.
8. **Substitute goods:** substitute goods are the goods that can be used in place of particular goods such as tea and coffee. If the price of a particular commodity increases, the demand of its substitute goods will increase. For example, if the price coffee increases, the demand of coffee will decrease but the demand of tea will increase.
9. **Independent goods:** independent goods are the goods that are not related with each other such as furniture, cloth; medicine etc. price of any of these commodities does not affect the demand of other commodities.
10. **Demand for consumer goods:** demand for consumer goods means the demand of goods and services that are demanded by ultimate consumers. These goods and services that are supposed to satisfy human wants directly such as food, cloths, etc. demand of consumer goods can again be divided into two parts: i.e. durable and non-durable consumer goods.
11. **Durable goods:** are the goods that are used for a long time such as furniture, TV etc. and are used again and again in the process of consumption.

12. **Non-durable goods:** are the goods that can be used only for one time in the process of consumption such as milk, egg, medicine etc.
13. **Collective demand:** when a particular goods and services is demanded for a number of uses, it is called collective demand. For example: demand of electricity is a collective demand.

5.5.4. Determinants of demand or factors affecting demand

- **Factors affecting the demand of consumer goods:** the goods which are used for the direct satisfaction of human wants. The factors which affect the demand are given as under.
- **Income of the consumer:** Consumers of high income group demand more of these goods than the consumers of low income group. Demand of these goods increases on an increase in the income of consumers and vice versa.
- **Price of the commodities:** Higher the prices of goods, less will be their demand and vice-versa. Demand of a commodity decreases on an increase in price and increases on a fall in price.
- **Habits and tastes:** If a consumer is habitual of a particular commodity or a particular brand, he will purchase more of it.
- **Size of population:** More the population, more will be demand of goods because the level of industrial activities depends directly upon the size of population of country.
- **Life period of goods:** The life period of goods affect the demand of these goods in two ways. Higher the life period of goods, more will be the confidence with which the consumers can buy them. Higher the life period of goods, less will be the demand.
- **Probability of technical advancement:** On technical advancement, the demand of new goods increases and that of outdated goods decreases.
- **Social customs:** If a particular commodity is a part of social customs and conventions, demand of it will be more.
- **Effects of advertisement and demonstration:** If a commodity is properly advertised and demonstrated, it becomes popular among consumers and as result, its demand increases.
- **Government policies:** If the government is promoting capital investment in the country, demand of capital goods will increase.

6

Utility Theory

6.1. Concept of Utility

In the ordinary language, 'utility' means 'usefulness'. In Economics, utility is defined as the power of a commodity or a service to satisfy a human want. Utility is a subjective or psychological concept. The same commodity or service gives different utilities to different people. For a vegetarian, mutton has no utility. Warm clothes have little utility for the people in hot countries. So utility is determined by the consumer and his need for the commodity.

Total Utility

Total Utility is denoted by the sum of utilities of all units of a commodity consumed. For example, if a consumer consumes ten biscuits, then the total utility is the sum of satisfaction of consuming all the ten biscuits.

Marginal Utility

Marginal Utility is the addition made to the total utility by consuming one more unit of a commodity. For example, if a consumer consumes 10 biscuits, the marginal utility of 10th unit is nothing but the total utility of 10 biscuits minus the total utility of 9 biscuits.

6.2. Law Of Diminishing Marginal Utility

The law of diminishing marginal utility explains an ordinary experience of a consumer. If a consumer takes more units of a commodity, the additional utility he derives from an extra unit of the commodity goes on falling. Thus, according to this law, the marginal utility decreases with the increase in the consumption of a commodity. When marginal utility decreases, the total utility increases at a diminishing rate.

Definition According to Marshall, "*The additional benefit which a person derives from a given increase of his stock of a thing diminishes with every increase in the stock that he already has*".

Explanation

Suppose Mr. X is hungry and eats apple one by one. The first apple gives him great pleasure (higher utility) as he is hungry; when he takes the second apple, the extent of his hunger will reduce. Therefore he will derive less utility from the second apple. If he continues to take additional apples, the utility derived from the third apple will be less than that of the second one. In this way, the additional utility (marginal utility) from the extra units will go on decreasing. If the consumer continues to take more apples, marginal utility falls to zero and then becomes negative.

For example, the utility derived by a person from successive units of consumption of apples is as under.

Units of apple	Total Utility	Marginal utility
1	20	20
2	35	15
3	45	10
4	50	5
5	50	0
6	45	-5
7	35	-10

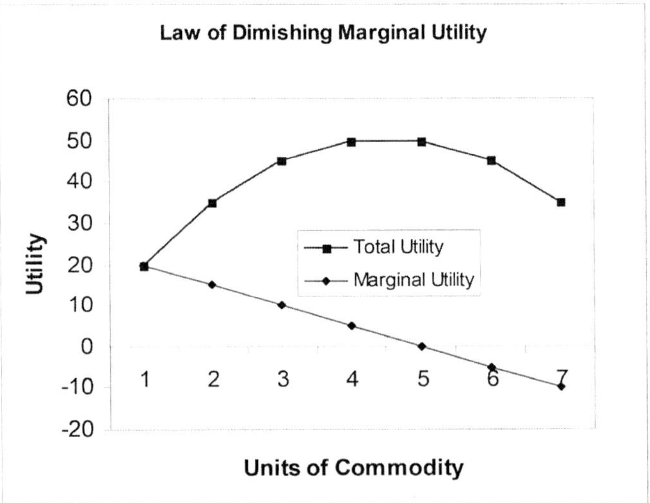

From the above table and figure, it is very clear that the marginal utility (addition made to the total utility) goes on declining. The consumer derives 20 units of utility from the first apple he consumes. When he consumes the apples continuously, the marginal utility falls to 5 units for the fourth apple and becomes zero for the fifth apple. The marginal utilities are negative for the 6th and 7th apples. Thus when the consumer consumes a commodity continuously, the marginal utility declines, reaches zero and then becomes negative.

Total utility, which is the sum of the utilities of all consumed units, initially increases but eventually begins to decline. As long as marginal utility is decreasing but remains positive, total utility continues to rise. For the first four units of an apple, total utility increases from 20 to 50 units. When marginal utility becomes zero (at the 5th apple), total utility reaches its maximum and remains constant at 50 units. However, once marginal utility turns negative (at the 6th and 7th apples), total utility starts to decrease, falling from 50 to 45 units and then to 35 units.

Relationship between Total Utility and Marginal Utility

S. No.	Total Utility	Marginal Utility
1	Increases	Declines
2	Reaches maximum	Reaches zero
3	Declines	Becomes negative

Importance

1. The Law of Diminishing Marginal Utility (DMU) serves as the basis for several economic principles. For instance, the Law of Demand is a direct outcome of the DMU. In simpler terms, as a consumer continues to consume more units of a commodity, the marginal utility derived from each additional unit decreases. This decline in utility, driven by the DMU, leads consumers to be willing to pay only a lower price for subsequent units.
2. The Law of Diminishing Marginal Utility (DMU) also applies to money. A wealthy individual already has a substantial amount of money, so as more money is added to their income, its marginal utility gradually decreases. However, Alfred Marshall assumed that the marginal utility of money remains constant.
3. This law is a handy tool for the Finance Minister for increasing tax rate on the rich.
4. Producers are guided by the operation the Law of DMU, unconsciously. They constantly change the design, the package of their goods so that the goods become more attractive to the consumers and they appear as 'new goods'. Or else, the consumers would think that they are using the same commodity, over and over. In such a situation, the Law of DMU operates in the minds of the consumers. Demand for such commodities may fall.

Assumptions

1. The units of consumption should be measured in standard quantities, such as a cup of tea or a bottle of a soft drink.
2. All units of the commodity should be identical in every aspect, including taste, quality, color, and size.
3. The law applies only if the consumption process continues without any interruption or time gap.
4. The consumer's taste, habits, and preferences must remain unchanged throughout the consumption process.
5. The income of the consumer remains constant.
6. The prices of the commodity consumed and its substitutes are constant.
7. The consumer is believed to be a rational economic man. As a rational consumer, he wants to maximize the total utility
8. Utility is measurable.

Criticism / Limitations

1. Deriving utility is a psychological experience, when we say a unit of X gives ten units of utility, this means that utility can be measured precisely. In reality, utility cannot be measured. For example, when a person sees a film and says it is very good, we cannot measure the utility he has derived from it. However, we can measure utility indirectly by the cinema fare he is willing to pay.
2. The Law is based on a single commodity consumption mode. That is, a consumer consumes only one good at a time. This is an unrealistic assumption. In real life, a consumer consumes more than one good at a time.
3. According to the Law, a consumer should consume successive units of the same good continuously. In real life it is not so.
4. The law assumes that the marginal utility of money remains constant, even when the amount of money changes. However, in reality, the marginal utility gained from consuming a good cannot be precisely measured in monetary terms.
5. Since utility varies from person to person, the marginal utility obtained from consuming a good cannot be measured with absolute precision.

6.3 Law of Equi – Marginal Utility

This law is also known as the law of substitution. "The law implies that if a person has a thing which he can put to several uses, he will distribute it between those uses in such a way that it has the same marginal utility in all" (Marshall). A consumer generally is confronted with the problem of buying from among several goods and services, given his limited income. He is left with the choice making, regarding purchase of commodities and their quantities so that the purchases that are decided upon ensure him maximum satisfaction. Here, the consumer aims at maximizing total utility by consuming possible goods and services given the income constraint. In this process the consumer substitutes the goods having greater utility for those which have lesser utility. This process is continued till the marginal utilities of the commodities purchased are equalized. Hence the name, the law of equi-marginal utility.

Assumptions

Before explaining the law, the following assumptions are made.

1. The consumer behaves rationally.
2. He has full knowledge about the commodities, their attributes, prices, etc., in the market.
3. Utility is measurable cardinally in terms of utils.
4. Commodities that are chosen are divisible and substitutable.

Explanation of the Law

Given the income constraint, the consumer makes prudent decisions in his purchases such that the allocation so made ensures him maximum satisfaction. Suppose the consumer has ₹25 to spend and can choose between three vegetables: potato, tomato, and ridge gourd. The marginal utilities derived from consuming these vegetables and the corresponding expenditures are shown in a table. Each unit of money (₹5) spent yields different marginal utilities. For instance, spending ₹5 on potatoes provides a marginal utility of 19 utils, the second ₹5 gives 16 utils, the third ₹5 gives 14 utils, and so on. To maximize satisfaction, the consumer must allocate the ₹25 so that the marginal utility of the last unit of money spent is equal across all choices. Based on the given marginal utilities, the consumer should allocate three units to tomatoes, one unit to potatoes, and one unit to ridge gourd. The total utility through this combination would be 100 (22 + 21 + 20 + 19 + 18). No other combination of vegetables gives as high as 100 utils.

No. of units (Rs. 5 per unit)	Marginal utilities per unit of Rs. 5		
	Potato	Tomato	Ridge gourd
1	19*	22*	18*
2	16	21*	17
3	14	20*	15
4	10	16	12
5	5	14	11

* Indicates units of money spent on vegetables

This combination remains optimal until there is a change in the consumer's income, preferences, or the prices of the goods. This law is also known as the **Principle of Proportionality**, as the consumer distributes their expenditure in a way that ensures the marginal utilities of the goods purchased are proportional to their prices. The concept of consumer equilibrium, where the consumer maximizes satisfaction within their budget, is illustrated below:

$$\frac{MU\ of\ X}{Price\ of\ X} = \frac{MU\ of\ Y}{Price\ of\ Y} = \frac{MU\ of\ Z}{Price\ of\ Z} = K$$

Practical Importance of Law of Equi –marginal Utility

1. **Consumption:** A rational consumer adheres to this law when planning their expenditure. They allocate their spending in such a way that the marginal utility obtained from each unit of money is nearly equal across all the goods they purchase.
2. **Production:** A rational producer allocates his limited resources among various possible enterprises in such a way that the marginal value product derived from each unit of resource on various enterprises are the same.
3. **Marketing:** The consumer should ensure that the marginal utility of a commodity is equal to its price when making purchases. This law helps guide consumers in efficiently allocating their available money across different goods to maximize overall utility
4. **Distribution:** The share of each factor of production is determined on the basis of marginal value productivity.
5. **Prices:** When the price of a commodity goes up in view of shortfall in supply, consumer prefers that commodity which is relatively less scarce. This preference of consumer brings down the price of the commodity.

Limitations of the Law

It needs a very careful scrutiny by the consumer regarding prices of various commodities and their substitutes. More often, the expenditure pattern is influenced by the habits, except in the case of very high priced goods for which certain amount of thinking goes before taking buying decisions. Another limitation for the operation of the law is indivisibility of certain goods which would not permit the equalization of marginal utilities. Further, it is possible that buying decisions are influenced by advertisement in which case rationality criterion may not be followed.

6.4. Consumer Equilibrium

The term *Consumer's equilibrium* refers to the quantity of goods and services a consumer can purchase based on their income and the prevailing market prices. The consumer's goal is to maximize satisfaction within their financial constraints. Simply put, consumer equilibrium is the point at which a consumer achieves the highest possible utility from their purchases, given their income and the prices of goods. A consumer is in equilibrium when the marginal utility per unit of money spent on each good is equal.

6.5. Derivation of Demand Curve

The law of demand, or the demand curve, can be understood through the Law of Diminishing Marginal Utility. This principle states that as a consumer acquires additional units of a good, its marginal utility—when measured in monetary terms—gradually declines. Essentially, the marginal utility curve slopes downward. A consumer continues purchasing the good until its marginal utility aligns with the market price, ensuring maximum satisfaction. This relationship demonstrates that diminishing marginal utility results in a downward-sloping demand curve, indicating that as the price of a good falls, consumers tend to purchase more. In the corresponding figure, the declining marginal utility of the good is depicted in monetary terms..

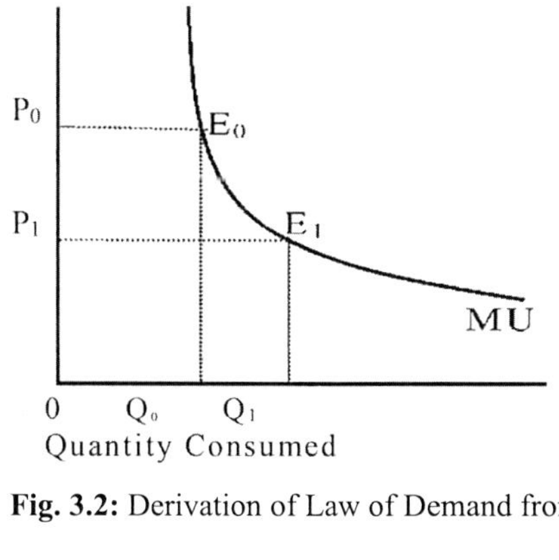

Fig. 3.2: Derivation of Law of Demand from Law of Diminishing Marginal Utility

Suppose the price of a good is **OP_0**, and the consumer reaches equilibrium by purchasing **OQ_0** units, where the marginal utility equals the given price **OP_0**. If the price drops to **OP_1**, the consumer increases their purchase to **OQ_1**, shifting equilibrium from **E_0 to E_1**. To align marginal utility with the new lower price **OP_1**, the consumer must buy more of the good. This demonstrates the inverse relationship between the quantity demanded and the price of the good, which is the foundation of the law of demand.

7

Consumer's Surplus

7.1. Introduction

The concept of consumer's surplus was first introduced by Alfred Marshall. When a consumer plans to buy a commodity, they assess the utility they will gain from its consumption. A rational consumer always compares the utility derived from a good with the price they must pay for it. If the utility exceeds the price, the consumer chooses to buy it; otherwise, they do not. The excess utility gained over the price paid is known as consumer's surplus.

In nutshell, Consumer's surplus is the difference between the amount a consumer is **willing to pay** for a good and the amount they **actually pay**.

Consumer's surplus = Price that a consumer is willing to pay - Price he actual pays

Suppose a consumer wants to buy a shirt and is willing to pay ₹250 for it, but the actual price is only ₹200. In this case, the consumer gains a surplus of ₹50. This difference, known as consumer's surplus, represents the extra benefit the consumer receives from the purchase.

Consumer's surplus is often experienced with commodities that are highly useful but relatively inexpensive, such as newspapers, salt, matchboxes, and postage stamps. In these cases, consumers are willing to pay more than the actual price, resulting in a surplus of utility

Estimation of Consumer's surplus

Units of apple	Marginal utility	Actual Price of Apple	Consumer's surplus
1	20	5	15
2	15	5	10
3	10	5	5
4	5	5	0
Total Units Purchased = 4	Total Utility = 50	Total Money Spent = Rs. 20	Consumer's Surplus = Rs.30

Marginal utility determines the price a consumer is willing to pay for a unit of a commodity, but as more units are purchased, marginal utility declines, reducing the price the consumer is willing to pay. The difference between marginal utility and the actual market price represents consumer's surplus. From the given table, consumer's surplus for each unit is calculated as the marginal utility minus the market price. For all units combined, consumer's surplus is found by subtracting the total amount spent from the total utility, i.e., ₹50 – ₹20 = ₹30.

A rise in the market price reduces the consumer's surplus and *vice-versa.* If price of apple increases to Rs. 10, consumer will buy only 3 units and in such case consumer's surplus will be decreased to Rs. 15 only.

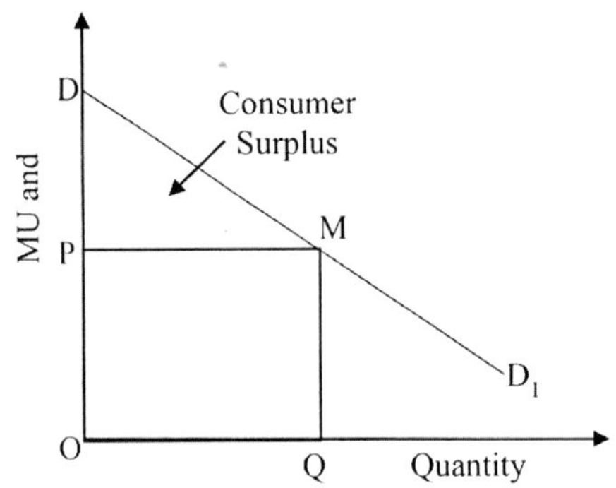

In the above figure, MU represents the marginal utility curve, OP is the price, and OM is the quantity purchased. For OM units, the consumer is willing to pay OAEM, but the actual amount paid is OPEM. Thus, the consumer's surplus is calculated as OAEM – OPEM = PAE (the shaded area). An increase in the market price reduces the consumer's surplus, as the gap between what the consumer is willing to pay and what they actually pay narrows.

7.2. Assumptions

1. Cardinal utility refers to the measurement of a commodity's utility in monetary terms.
2. Marshall assumes a clear relationship between the **anticipated satisfaction** (utility) and the **actual satisfaction** (realized utility).
3. Marginal utility of money is constant
4. Absence of differences in income, tastes, fashion etc.
5. Independent goods and independent utilities.
6. The demand for a commodity is influenced solely by its price, excluding other factors that affect demand.

7.3. Criticism / Limitations

Two major criticisms against the Marshallian concept of Consumer's Surplus are:

1. Marshall assumed that utility can be quantified or measured, but J.R.Hicks says that is immeasurable, because it is psychological in nature
2. The Marshallian assumption of marginal utility of money remaining constant. But it is unrealistic. The marginal utility of money rises as the stock of money decreases.

7.4. Importance of Consumer's Surplus

1. It is useful to the Finance Minister in formulating taxation policies.
2. It is helpful in fixing a higher price by a monopolist in the market, based on the extent of consumer's surplus enjoyed by consumers.
3. It enables comparison of the standard of living of people of different regions or countries. This comparison helps to distinguish consumption levels between the people, who are living in rich countries and poor countries. For example, a middleclass person in USA enjoys more consumers' surplus than a similar person in Uttar Pradesh.

8

Elasticity of Demand

8.1. Meaning

The Law of Demand states that when the price of a good increases, its quantity demanded decreases, assuming all other factors remain constant. However, the law does not specify how much the quantity demanded will decrease in response to a price increase or how sensitive demand is to price changes. This information is crucial for businesses and policymakers. To address this, Alfred Marshall developed the concept of elasticity of demand, which measures the responsiveness of quantity demanded to changes in factors such as price, income, and the price of related goods.

8.2. Type of Elasticity of Demand

There are three types of elasticity of demand viz., 01) Price Elasticity of Demand 02) Income Elasticity of Demand 03) Cross elasticity of Demand

1. Price elasticity of Demand

Price elasticity measures the responsiveness of the **quantity demanded** of a commodity to changes in its **price**, while keeping all other factors constant (**ceteris paribus**).

$$Price\,elasticity\,of\,Demand = \frac{Percentage\,change\,in\,quantity\,demand}{percentage\,change\,in\,price} \quad \text{or,}$$

$$Price\,elasticity\,of\,Demand = \frac{\Delta Q}{Q} \times \frac{P}{\Delta P}$$

Degree of Price elasticity of Demand

It is categorized into five parts;

i) Perfectly Elastic

- A slight change in price bring a tremendous change in quantity demanded.
- Elasticity of demand is infinite ($e_p = \infty$).
- The demand curve will be a horizontal line parallel to X-axis.
- It is mostly a theoretical concept.

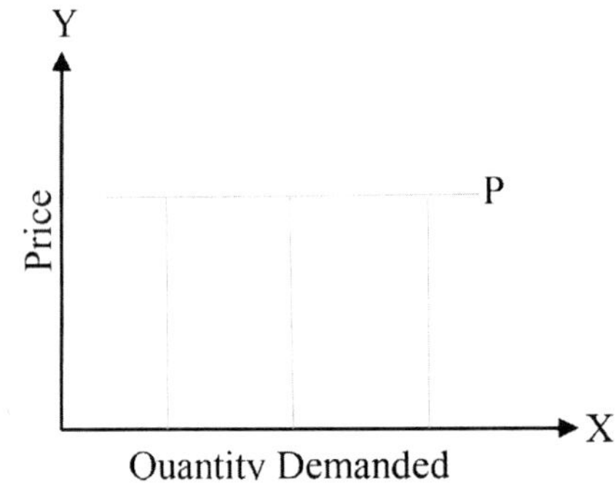

ii) Perfectly inelastic

- A change in price does not lead to any change in the quantity demanded.
- The price of commodity may increase or decrease but the quantity demanded remain same.
- Elasticity of demand is Zero (ep=o).
- The demand curve is vertical to to X-axis.
- It is a theoretical concept.
- It is clear from figure that a huge rise in price from P_1 to P_2 has no impact in quantity demand.

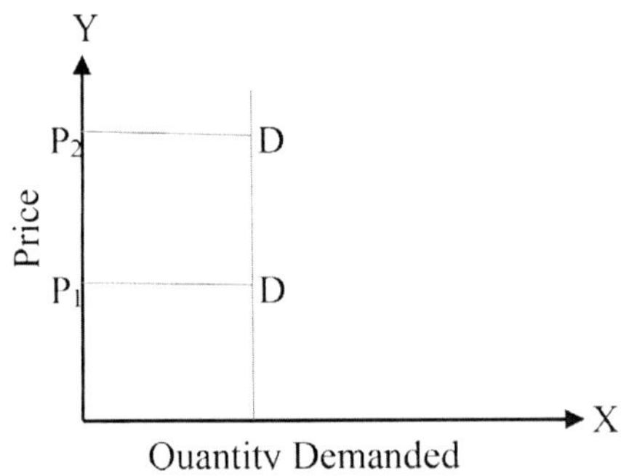

iii) Relatively Elastic

- Relatively elastic demand occurs when a slight change in price results in a significant change in quantity demanded.
- A slight proportional change in price leads to a significantly larger proportional change in demand, and vice versa.
- For example, if the price of gold decreases by **6%** and the quantity demanded rises by **20%**, the demand is considered relatively elastic.

- Elasticity of demand is greater than unity ($E_p > 1$).
- As illustrated in the figure, a small change in price from P_1 to P_2 results in a significantly larger change in demand from D_1 to D_2.

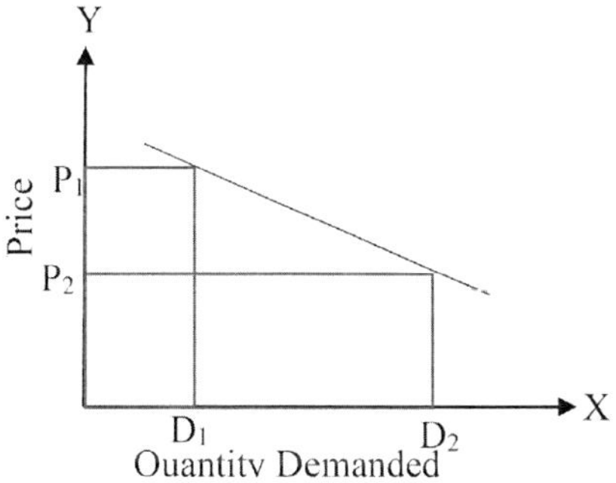

iv) Relatively Inelastic

- Under relatively inelastic demand, a certain percentage change in price leads to a smaller percentage change in quantity demanded.
- A large proportional decrease in price is followed by a smaller proportional increase in quantity demanded, and vice versa.
- Gasoline and salt are common examples of relatively inelastic products.
- Elasticity of demand is less than unity ($E_p < 1$)
- As shown in the figure, a significant change in **price** from **P_1 to P_2** results in a relatively small change in **quantity demanded** from **D_1 to D_2.**

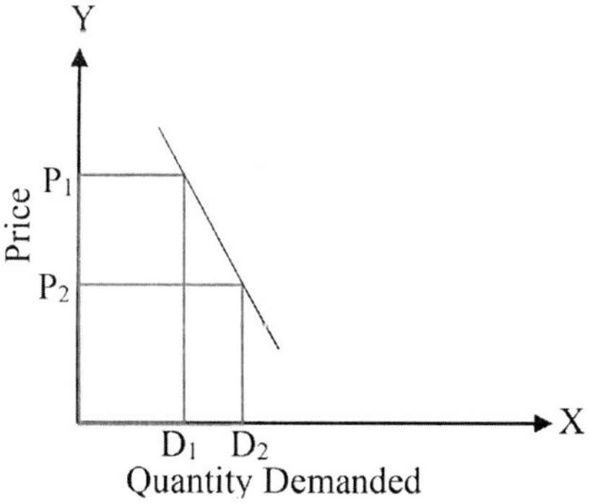

v) Unitary Elastic

- Demand is considered unitary elastic when a proportional change in price leads to an equal proportional change in quantity demanded.

- Elasticity of demand is one ($E_p=1$.)
- For example, a 10% increase in price causes a 10% decrease in demand quantity
- From figure it is clear that a change in price from P_1 to P_2 create similar change in quantity demanded from D_1 to D_2.

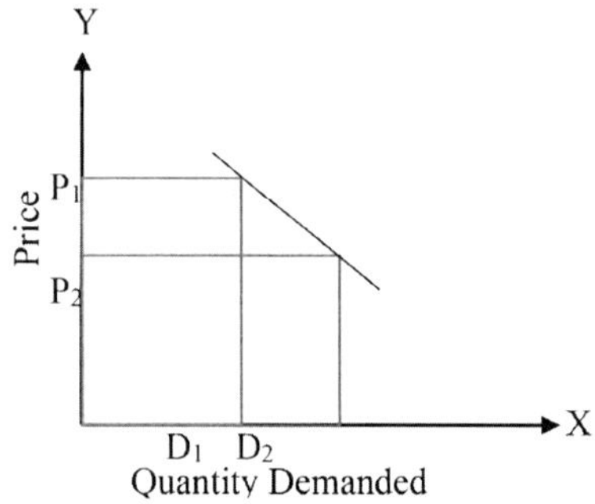

2. Income Elasticity of Demand

Income elasticity measure the responsiveness of quantity demanded due to change in income level of consumer when other factor of influencing are constant.

- For normal goods, Elasticity of demand is greater than zero ($Ey>0$).
- For inferior goods, Elasticity of demand is less than unity ($Ey<1$).
- For luxury/superior goods, Elasticity of demand is greater than unity ($Ey>1$).
- For necessities goods, Elasticity of demand is between zero to one($0<Ey<1$).

$$Income\,elasticity\,of\;Demand = \frac{Percentage\,change\,in\,quantity\,demand}{percentage\,change\,in\,income}$$

or,

$$Income\,elasticity\,of\;Demand = \frac{\Delta Q}{Q} \times \frac{Y}{\Delta Y}$$

3. Cross Elasticity of Demand

It measure the responsiveness of quantity demand for one good (x) in influenced by the price of other related good (y) i.e.,

- For substitute good Cross Elasticity of Demand is positive (+)
- For complement good Cross Elasticity of Demand is negative (-)

$$Cross\ elasticity\ of\ Demand = \frac{Percentage\ change\ in\ quantity\ demand\ of\ X}{Percentage\ change\ in\ price\ of\ related\ good\ Y}$$

or,

$$Cross\ elasticity\ of\ Demand = \frac{\Delta Qx}{Qx} \times \frac{Py}{\Delta Py}$$

8.3 Measurement of price elasticity of demand

a) Total outlay or expenditure methods
b) Point elasticity of Demand
c) Arc Elasticity of Demand

a) Total Outlay or experiment Method:

The elasticity of demand can be determined by analyzing how changes in price lead to corresponding changes in demand, which in turn affect the total expenditure on goods.

- If a change in price does not result in any variation in total expenditure, the demand is said to have **unitary elasticity**, where $\mathbf{e_p = 1}$.
- If price and total revenue have an inverse relationship—meaning total revenue decreases when price increases and rises when price decreases—demand is considered **elastic**, with $\mathbf{e_p > 1}$.
- When price and total revenue move in the same direction—meaning total revenue increases with a price rise and decreases with a price fall—demand is considered **inelastic**, with $\mathbf{e_p < 1}$.

b) Point elasticity of Demand

The point elasticity method was given by Alfred Marshall It is a geometrical method for measuring the elasticity at a point on the demand curve. A straight line demand curve joining the two axes in considered, showing the measurement of point elasticity. Elasticity at any point on the demand curve is the ratio of the lower part of the straight line to the upper point. The various values of elasticity as shown in the graph below:

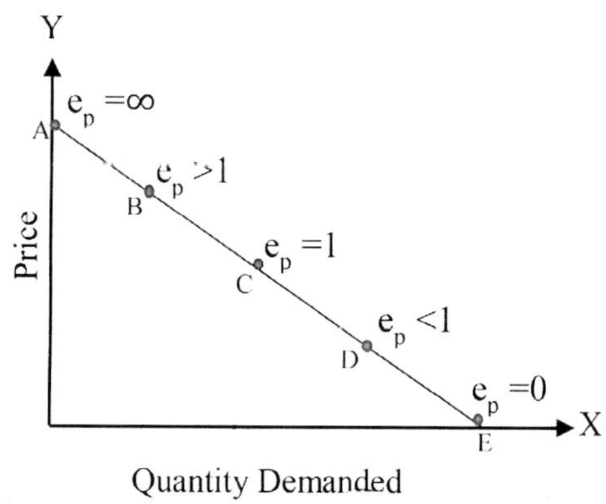

Formula to find out Ep through point method is,

$$E_p = \frac{\text{Lower segment of the demand curve}}{\text{Upper segment of the demand curve}}$$

For example, in above figure, the length of the demand curve AB is 4 cm.

At point E, Ep = EB/EA = 2/2 = 1 (Ep=1, i.e., Unitary elastic demand)

At point C, Ep = CB/CA = 3/1 = 3 (Ep>1, i.e., Elastic demand)

At point D, Ep = DB/DA = 1/3 = 0.33 (Ep<1, i.e., Inelastic demand)

At point A, Ep = AB/0 = 4/0 = Infinite (Ep=α, i.e. Perfectly elastic demand)

At point B, Ep = 0/BA = 0/4 = 0 (Ep=0, i.e. Perfectly inelastic demand)

c) Arc elasticity of Demand

The price elasticity of demand measure between two distinct point on demand curve is called arc elasticity of demand. This method uses the midpoint between the old and new data in the case of price and quantity. It studies a portion of the demand curve between two point. An arc is segment or a portion of a curved line. Arc elasticity is employed in order to compute price elasticity coefficient from the discrete data. The following formula is used to compute arc elasticity.

$$E_d = \frac{\dfrac{Q_1 - Q_2}{\dfrac{Q_1 + Q_2}{2}}}{\dfrac{P_1 - P_2}{\dfrac{P_1 + P_2}{2}}} = \frac{\dfrac{\Delta Q}{(Q_1 + Q_2)}}{\dfrac{\Delta P}{(P_1 + P_2)}}$$

Where, Q_1 stands for the first quantity observed and Q_2 for second quantity. Similar, P_1 is the first observed price and P_2 is the second price.

9

Production

9.1. Production

Production means creation of value in the goods, i. e. creation of utility. Production activity helps in transforming a set of inputs into goods and services. It essentially means transforming of one set of goods into another. The output generated from production possesses greater utility than the combined inputs used in the production process. The inputs that are utilized in production of goods may be provided by the nature and/ or by other industries.

9.2. Factors of Production

These mean the production resources required to produce a given product. Fraser defined factor of production as "a group or class of original productive resources". The factors of production have been traditionally classified as land, labour, capital and organization.

Land

According to Marshall, land means "the materials and forces which nature gives freely for man's aid, in land and water, in air and light and heat." In Economics the term land has a very broad meaning. It includes all free gifts of nature available to mankind *viz.*, air, water and land. It includes all types of land surfaces such as mountains, valley, plains, forests etc. It includes all types of water resources such as rivers, oceans, etc. Thus the concept of land includes all natural resources on, above and below the earth's surface.

Labour

The term, labour has wide and diversified meaning in economics. It can be physical work or mental work that is done by a person with an aim of earning money. It includes the work done by farmers, workers, the service of teachers, doctors, actors, etc. In the words of Marshall, labour is defined as "any exertion of mind or body undergone partly or wholly with a view to earn some good other than the pleasure derived directly from the work". Any work that is done for pleasure does not come under labour.

Characteristics of Labour

1. Labour is inseparable from labourer.
2. Labour is perishable.
3. Labour has very weak bargaining power.
4. Lack of free mobility.
5. Supply of labour is independent of demand.
6. Supply of labour peculiarly changes with the wages.

Capital

Capital is not a natural factor like land; rather, it is the outcome of human effort. It consists of man-made goods used to produce other goods and services. Examples of capital goods include machinery, raw materials, transport equipment, and dams. Capital serves as a produced means of production. According to Karl Marx, capital is "crystallized labor." While all capital qualifies as wealth, not all wealth qualifies as capital. Money becomes capital only when it is invested in purchasing capital goods. For instance, residential buildings are considered personal wealth but are not classified as capital.

Characteristics of Capital

1. Capital is not a free gift of nature. It is the result of man – made efforts. Machinery, implements, etc., are considered as capital goods.
2. Capital is productive because it contributes to increasing the overall efficiency of all resources used in the production process
3. It is also prospective as its accumulation rewards income in future.
4. Capital is highly mobile as it possesses the characteristic of territorial mobility.
5. Capital is **supply elastic** since its availability can be adjusted based on demand.

Organization

In any business activity, there is always an individual who oversees and manages its operations. This person coordinates and regulates all the factors involved in the business while also taking responsibility for its outcomes. Such an individual is known as an **entrepreneur** (or **organizer**), and the business activity they undertake is referred to as an **enterprise** or **organization**. The success of an organization largely depends on the skills and capabilities of the entrepreneur. By efficiently allocating resources, the entrepreneur can maximize productivity, ensuring optimal use of available inputs. Therefore, the success or failure of an enterprise is directly influenced by the entrepreneur's role in the business. Below are the key functions of an entrepreneur.

Functions of Entrepreneur

1. Identification and initiation: Entrepreneur is the person who identifies a particular business activity and initiates the idea of commencing the business.
2. Location of the enterprise: The place where the business unit is proposed to be set up is finalized by the entrepreneur.
3. Organizing
4. Supervision
5. Introduction of innovation
6. Risk taking

9.3. Production Function

- **The functional relationship between inputs and outputs is known as production function.**
- It expresses the relationship between **quantity** of output and the quantities of various inputs used in production.
- It shows the **maximum amount of production** that can be produced from a given set of inputs in the existing state of technology or the **minimum quantities of various inputs** required to produce a given quantity.
- The **production function** can be expressed as under:

$$Y = f(X_1, X_2, X_3, \ldots, X_n).$$

Where, Y = quantity produced during a given period of time;

$X_1, X_2, X_3, \ldots, X_n$ = quantities of different factors used in production.

9.3.1. Definition

Production function is a technical and mathematical relationship describing the manner and extent to which a particular product depends upon the quantities of inputs or services of inputs, used at a given level of technology and in a given period of time.

9.3.2 Types of Production Function

There are two types of production function

(1) Short-run production function and

(2) Long-run production function

1. Short-run production function

It examines the relationship between **one variable factor** and output, keeping the quantities of **other factors fixed**.

It is also called **The law of variable proportions**

a. Single Variable Production Function

$Y = f(X_1 \mid X_2, X_3, \ldots, X_n)$.

Where, Y = output;

X_1 = variable input;

$X_2, X_3, \ldots, X_n$ = fixed inputs.

b. Two Variable Production Function

$Y = f(X_1, X_2 \mid X_3, X_4, \ldots, X_n)$.

Where, Y = output;

X_1 and X_2 = variable inputs;

$X_3, X_4, \ldots, X_n$ = fixed inputs.

2. Long-run production function

- In the long run, **all factors can be changed**. This production function studies the changes in output when all factors or inputs are changed.
- It is also called **Returns to scale**.
- An increase in scale means that all inputs or factors are increased in the **same proportion** i.e, double, triple, etc.

10

Law of Return

10.1. Introduction

In the production process, the farmers combine the required input factor in various proportion. This type of usage of input by the farmer gives way for the operation of law of returns. In the production process, when the single input factor is varied keeping other required factor constant, the relationship take place between single variable input and the consequent output pertain to either one or a combination of the following relationship.

1. Law of increasing returns;
2. Law of constant returns; and
3. Law of decreasing returns.

10.1.1. Law of increasing returns

According to the **law of increasing returns**, each additional (or marginal) unit of input leads to a proportionally larger increase in output compared to the previous unit. In other words, the productivity of inputs rises as more units are employed.

Seed (x)	Output (y)	Additional input ()	Additional input ()	Marginal rate of return $= \frac{\Delta y}{\Delta x}$
5	2.00	5	2.0	$\frac{2.0}{5} = 0.40$
10	4.40	5	2.4	$\frac{2.4}{5.0} = 0.48$
15	7.50	5	3.1	$\frac{3.1}{5.0} = 0.62$
20	11.30	5	3.8	$\frac{3.8}{5.0} = 0.76$
25	18.00	5	6.7	$\frac{6.7}{5.0} = 1.34$

Each successive unit add more to the output then the previous one the rate of change or marginal productivity . The ratio of will go on increasing more and more unit of input are added i.e.,

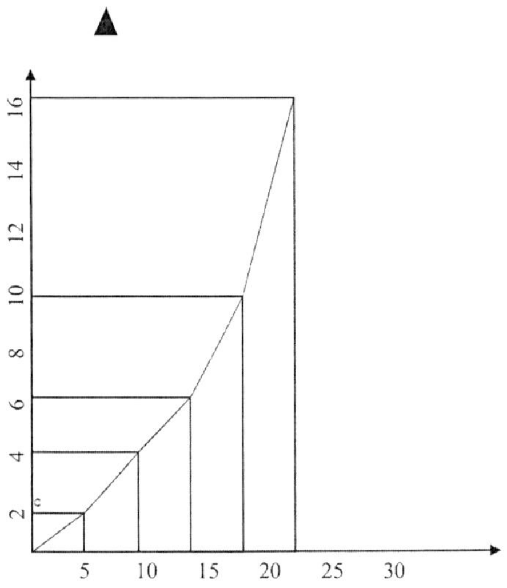

Fig. 10.1.1: Law of increasing returns

10.1.2. Law of constant returns

Under **constant returns**, each additional unit of a variable input, when applied to a fixed factor, results in the same increase in output. This means the additional product remains constant for every extra unit of input used.

Seed (x)	Output (y)	Additional input ()	Additional input ()	Marginal rate of return $= \frac{\Delta y}{\Delta x}$
5	2	5	2	$\frac{2.0}{5} = 0.40$
10	4	5	2	$\frac{2.0}{5} = 0.40$
15	6	5	2	$\frac{2.0}{5} = 0.40$
20	8	5	2	$\frac{2.0}{5} = 0.40$
25	10	5	2	$\frac{2.0}{5} = 0.40$

At any point on the line the slope is determine by $\frac{\Delta y}{\Delta x}$. The production function had the same slope throughout its entire range express as

$$\frac{\Delta y_1}{\Delta x_1}=\frac{\Delta y_2}{\Delta x_2}=\frac{\Delta y_3}{\Delta x_3}=\ldots\frac{\Delta y_n}{\Delta x_n}$$

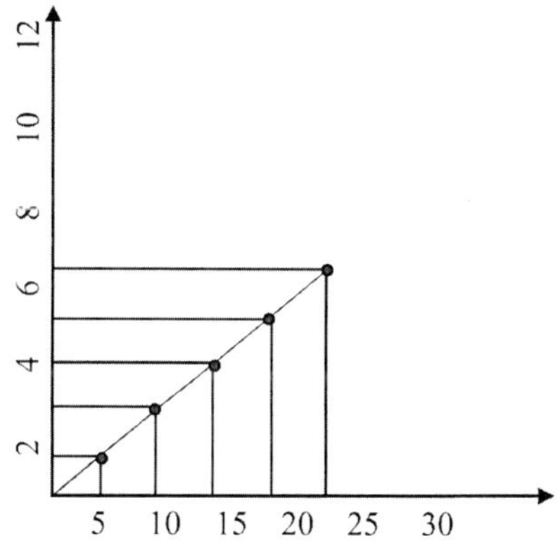

Fig. 10.1.2: Law of constant returns

10.1.3. Law of decreasing return

Each successive unit of input contributes less to the total output than the previous unit, meaning the additional output decreases with each extra unit of input. This phenomenon, known as the **law of diminishing returns**, is commonly observed in almost all practical agricultural scenarios.

Seed (x)	**Output (y)**	**Additional input (Δx)**	**Additional input (Δy)**	**Marginal rate of return =** $\frac{\Delta y}{\Delta x}$
5	2.0	5	2.0	$\frac{2.0}{5}=0.40$
10	3.5	5	1.8	$\frac{1.8}{5}=0.36$
15	5.2	5	1.4	$\frac{1.4}{5}=0.28$
20	6.3	5	1.1	$\frac{1.1}{5}=0.22$
25	6.9	5	0.6	$\frac{0.6}{5}=0.12$

The ratio of $\frac{\Delta y}{\Delta x}$ will go on decreasing as more as more unit of input are added i.e.,

$$\frac{\Delta y_1}{\Delta x_1} > \frac{\Delta y_2}{\Delta x_2} > \frac{\Delta y_3}{\Delta x_3} > \ldots \frac{\Delta y_n}{\Delta x_n}$$

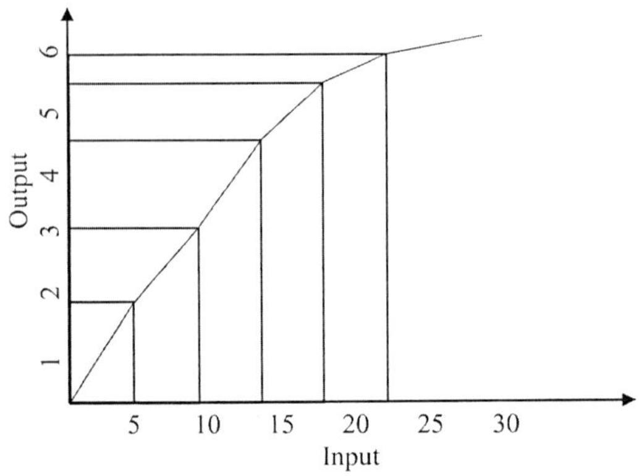

Fig. 10.1.3: Law of decreasing return

11

Input- Output Relationship/ Law of Variable Proportion

11.1. Introduction

The input-output relationship is commonly referred to as the Classical Production Function.

The Classical Production Function is also known as the Law of Diminishing Returns or the Law of Increasing Costs.

It is sometimes termed the "Law of Life", as it serves as a fundamental principle of economics upon which several other economic laws are based.

This law analyzes the relationship between a single variable factor and output while keeping all other factors constant.

It represents a short-run production function.

11.2. Definition

The Law of Increasing Cost states that the proportion of one factor in a combination of factors increases till a certain point but after that first the marginal product then the average product will diminish.

According to Marshall "*An increase in capital and labour applied in the cultivation of land causes in general less than proportionate increase in the amount of produce raised, unless it happens to coincide with the improvements in the arts of agriculture*".

According to Earl O. Heady "*If the quantity of one of productive service is increased by equal increments, with the quantity of other resource services held constant, the increments to total product may increase at first but will decrease after certain point*".

11.3. Production Function used

$Y = f(X_1 \mid X_2, X_3, \ldots, X_n)$.

Where

Y = output;

X_1 = variable input;

X_2, X_3, ...X_n = fixed inputs.

11.4. Objective

- The primary goal of this relationship is to ensure the optimal utilization of resources for maximum efficiency.
- The key management challenge in this analysis is determining the optimal level of production.

11.5. Limitations

The law of diminishing returns does not apply in certain situations which is also known as limitations of the law. The limitations are:

1. Improved methods of cultivation
2. New soils and
3. Insufficient capital.

11.6. Example

Input (X)	Output (TP) (Y)	Marginal Input (ΔX)	Marginal Output (ΔY)	AP (Y/X)	MP (ΔY/ΔX)	Remarks
0	0	-	-	-	-	Increasing at increasing rate
1	2	1	2	2.00	2	
2	5	1	3	2.50	3	
3	9	1	4	3.00	4	
4	14	1	5	3.50	5	Increasing at constant rate
5	19	1	5	3.80	5	
6	23	1	4	3.83	4	Increasing at decreasing rate
7	26	1	3	3.71	3	
8	28	1	2	3.50	2	
9	29	1	1	3.22	1	
10	29	1	0	2.90	0	
11	28	1	-1	2.54	-1	Decreasing (negative return)
12	26	1	-2	2.16	-2	

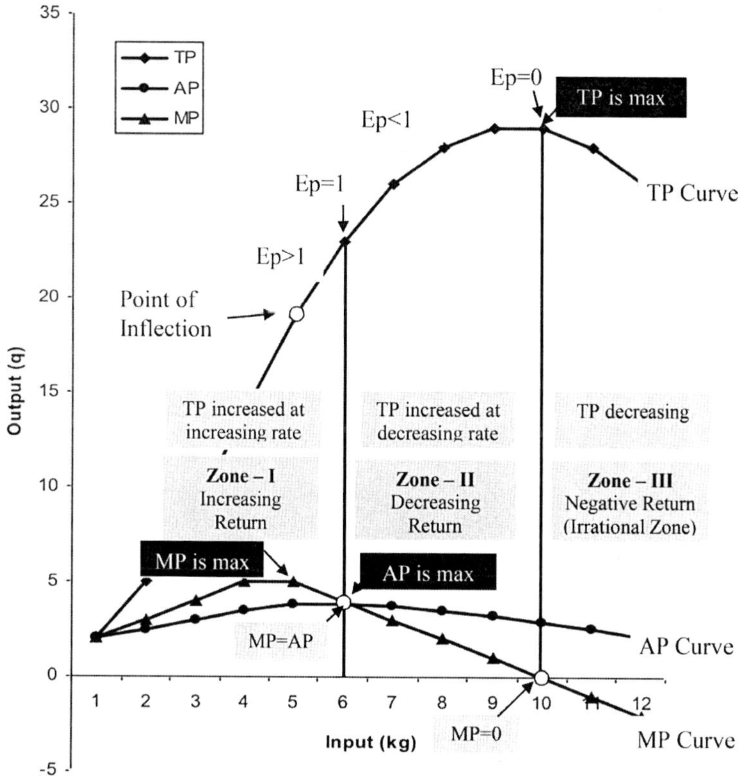

Fig. 11.6: Classical Production Function

Behavior of TP Curve	Behavior of MP Curve	Behavior of AP Curve
Initially, TP increasing at increasing rate TP increasing at decreasing rate TP riches at maximum when MP = 0 and remains constant TP decreasing	MP increasing MP attains maximum MP remains constant MP decreasing	AP increasing At MP = AP, AP attains maximum AP is decreasing

A. Relationship between TP and MP

When TP increasing at increasing rate, MP also increasing.

When TP increasing at decreasing rate, MP also decreasing.

When TP is maximum or remain constant, MP=0

When TP decreasing, MP becomes negative.

When TP changes its curvature (from increasing rate to decreasing rate), MP is maximum. This point is referred to as point of inflection.

B. Relation between MP and AP

- When MPP increases, APP also increases. As long as MPP remains higher than APP, APP continues to increase.
- When the MPP curve falls below the APP curve, APP begins to decline. In other words, when APP decreases, MPP is always lower than APP.
- APP reaches its maximum when MPP = APP. At this point, the MPP curve must intersect the APP curve from above at its highest point.

So when MP > AP AP↑

MP < AP AP↓

MP = AP AP is at maximum.

Relationship between MP and TP	Relationship between MP and AP
MP > 0, TP increasing	When MP > AP, AP increasing; Ep >1
MP = 0, TP maximum	When MP = AP, AP is maximum; Ep = 1
MP < 0, TP decreasing	When MP < AP, AP decreasing; Ep < 1

Three Zones of Production Function

The classical production function can be divided into three zones.

Zone-I: Stage of increasing returns

This region begins at the origin and extends up to the point where the average product reaches its highest (maximum) or where MP=AP.

During this stage, the TP, AP and MP are increasing.

It is worth noting that MP increases at first (Zone I) but later starts to decline (Zone II). However, even as it declines, MP remains greater than AP.

AP increases throughout this region indicating that the efficiency of all the variable inputs keeps on increasing.

Zone-II: Stage of decreasing returns

This region starts where 1st zone ends. i.e. MP=AP and extends to the point where MP=0 or TP is maximum.

In this zone, the TP continues to increase but at a diminishing rate.

The MP and the AP are declining but both are positive.

Zone-III: Stage of negative returns

This region starts when MP crosses zero and becomes negative.

In this zone the MP becomes negative.

The TP and the AP are declining.

Rational / Irrational Zones stage of production

Zone-III

This is a **irrational zone** because in this zone the TP is declining and MP becomes negative which signifies that additional quantities of inputs reduces the total output.

Therefore, operating in this region is not recommended, even if additional input quantities are available at free of cost.

If a farmer operates in this zone, he will have **double loss**: i.) reduced production and ii) unnecessarily additional cost of inputs.

For example, many farmers in **canal area** operate in this zone. They use excess water which ultimately reduces the profit.

Zone-I

This is also **irrational zone** because, the AP increases throughout this zone indicating that the efficiency of all the input variables keeps on increasing. So, farmer should not stop in this zone and he must produce up to the level where AP is maximum.

- Input-use should be continued until zone-II. Hence, **it is not logical to stop using the input** when its efficiency is still increasing. If he stops in this region, some of his resource will remain **unused or underutilized**.
- For example, most of the tribal farmers operate in Zone-I because they don't have sufficient inputs.

Zone-II

This is a **rational zone.**

In this zone, TP is increasing; MP is decreasing but remains positive.

The area of economic significance lies within the boundaries of Zone-II.

The ideal utilization of input falls within the range of this region, but its exact position can only be determined when input and output prices are known.

This zone represents the range of rational production decisions.

Summary

Zone - I	Zone - II	Zone – III
From origin to AP=MP	From AP=MP to MP=0	From MP=0 to onwards
Ep > 1	Ep < 1	Ep < 0
Irrational zone	Rational zone	Irrational zone
Stage of **increasing return**	Stage of **decreasing return**	Stage of **negative return**
TP, AP & MP all are increasing	TP is increasing but at a decreasing rate. MP & AP decreasing but are positive.	TP, AP & MP all are decreasing. MP becomes negative.
Zone of **underutilization** of resources	Zone of **optimum** level of resources	Zone of **overutilization** of resources
MR>MC	MR=MC	MR<MC
Fixed cost >Variable cost	Fixed cost= Variable cost	Fixed cost < Variable cost
Marginal Value product (MVP)> Marginal Input cost (MIC)	Marginal Value product (MVP)= Marginal Input cost (MIC)	Marginal Value product (MVP)< Marginal Input cost (MIC)

11.7. Optimum Level of Input use

Optimum level of output use will be at the stage where the Marginal Value product (MVP) and marginal input cost (MIC) are equal i.e., MVP=MIC.

Marginal Value product (MVP): It is the additional income received from an additional unit of input. It is computed using following formula.

$$MVP = \frac{change\,in\,total\,value\,product}{change\,in\,input\,level} = \frac{\Delta TR}{\Delta X} = MPP \times P_Q$$

Marginal Input Cost (MIC): It is defined as the change in total input cost by using an additional unit of input. It is expressed as:

$$MIC = \frac{change\,in\,total\,input\,cost}{change\,in\,input\,level} = \frac{\Delta TC}{\Delta X} = price\ per\,unit\,of\ input$$

To calculate optimum level,

Labour wage= Rs. 30/- Manday

Price per kg of output= Rs.5/-

Input	Total Physical product (TPP)	Marginal Physical Product (MPP)	Total value product (TVP)	Marginal Value product (MVP)	Marginal Input cost (MIC)
1	15		75		
2	38	23	190	115	30
3	66	28	330	140	30
4	96	30	480	150	30
5	120	24	600	120	30

Input	Total Physical product (TPP)	Marginal Physical Product (MPP)	Total value product (TVP)	Marginal Value product (MVP)	Marginal Input cost (MIC)
6*	126	6	630	30*	30*
7	126	0	630	0	30
8	120	-6	600	-30	30
9	90	-30	450	-150	30
10	50	-40	250	-200	30

*Optimum input level

11.8. Optimum Level of Output use

Optimum level of output use will be at the stage where the cost of additional input (MC) and the value of additional product (MR) are equal i.e., MC=MR.

Marginal Cost (MC): It is defined as additional cost incurred for producing an additional unit of output the expression is as follow:

$$MC = \frac{Change\,in\,total\,input\,cost}{Change\,in\,total\,physical\,product} = \frac{\Delta TC}{\Delta Q}$$

Marginal Revenue (MR): It is defined as the additional income obtained from producing one more unit of output. It is expressed as:

$$MR = \frac{Change\,in\,total\,income}{Change\,in\,total\,physical\,product} = \frac{\Delta TR}{\Delta Q}$$

To calculate optimum level, data regarding price of input as well as output will be required.

Suppose, price of input is **Rs.5/unit** and price of output is **Rs.4/unit.**

Input	Total Physical product (TPP)	Marginal Physical Product (MPP)	Total Revenue (TR)	Marginal Revenue (MR)	Marginal Cost (MC)
1	15		75		
2	38	23	190	5	1.30
3	66	28	330	5	1.07
4	96	30	480	5	1.0
5	120	24	600	5	1.25
6	126*	6	630	5*	5.0*
7	126	0	630	5	0
8	120	-6	600	5	-5.0
9	90	-30	450	5	-1.0
10	50	-40	250	5	-0.75

*optimum output level

11.9. Application of the Law

- The law is widely applicable to **agriculture**.
- Besides, agriculture, it also applies to **mining, fisheries** and also to **building industries** where **the nature has supremacy**.
- It is therefore, often remarked that the part that the **nature** plays in production corresponds to **diminishing returns** and the part which **man** plays conforms to the law of **increasing returns**.
- Thus, we can say that **agriculture,** where nature is supreme, is subject to **diminishing returns**, while **industry**, where man is supreme, is subject to **increasing returns**.

Reasons why agriculture is subject to the law of diminishing returns

- Agricultural is related to nature. Man is not a complete master of nature. The operations are likely to be interrupted frequently by rain and other climatic changes.
- The agricultural operations are spread out over a wide area, and consequently supervision cannot be very effective.
- Scope for the use of specialized machinery is also very limited.
- No scope for division of labour.

Reasons why industry is subject to the law of increasing returns

- In case of manufacturing industries, **man** has the fullest scope to show his ability.
- By the introduction of **division of labour** and the use of the most **modern technology**, production can be greatly increased.
- Concentration of workers under one roof renders **supervision easy and effective**.

But, if the industry is **expanded too much**, supervision will become difficult and the costs will go up. In such situation, **law of diminishing returns will set in**. A prudent industrialist may not allow that stage to come at all.

Hence, we can say that the law of diminishing returns has wide applications. In agriculture it sets in earlier, while in industry, it sets in a later stage.

12

Returns to Scale

12.1. Meaning

The rate at which output change as the quantity of all input are change. It is based on long run law in which all factor are variable and factor proportion do not change.

Stage of Return to Scale

1. Constant return to scale
2. Increasing return to scale
3. Decreasing return to scale

1. Constant return to scale

- In constant return, Change in proportion of input is equal to the change in proportion of output.
- A constant return to scale is also known as linear homogenous production function of the first degree.
- Example: Industry.

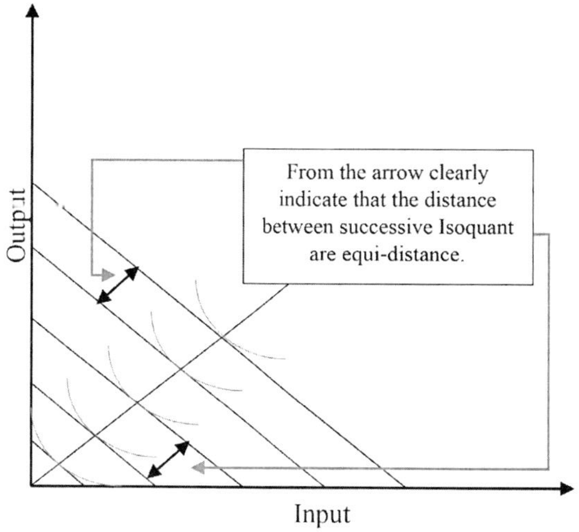

2. Increasing return to scale

In increasing return, the change in proportion of input is less than change in proportion of output.

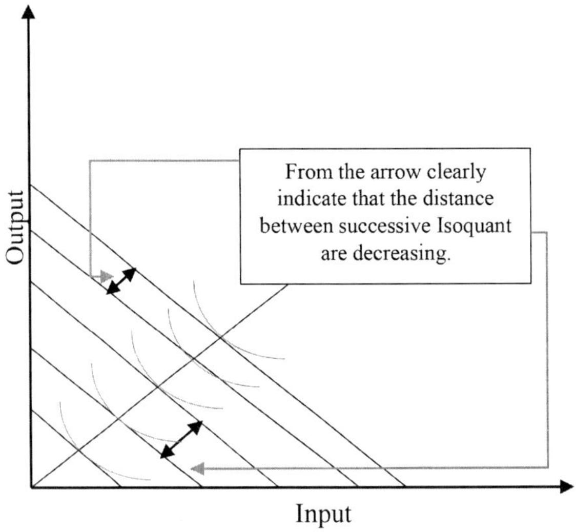

3. Decreasing return to scale

The change in proportion of input is greater than the change in proportion of output.

- Example: Agriculture

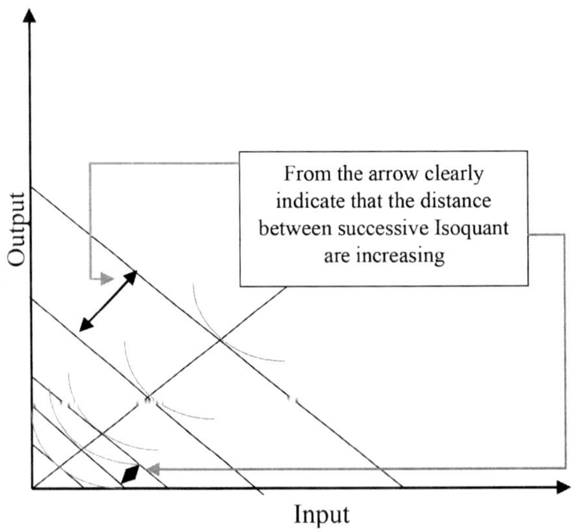

Note: The return to scale can also be obtained by using two variable Cobb-Douglas production function as:

$Y = AL^{\alpha} K^{\beta}$

Where

Y = Output,

A= Constant

L= Labour

K= Capital

α = elasticity coefficient of labour

β = elasticity coefficient of capital

Sum of Elasticity coefficient = $\sum^{n}_{(i=1)} \alpha + \beta$

- If the value of $\sum^{n}_{(i=1)} \alpha + \beta = 1$ represent constant return to scale
- If the value of $\sum^{n}_{(i=1)} \alpha + \beta > 1$ represent increasing return to scale
- If the value of $\sum^{n}_{(i=1)} \alpha + \beta < 1$ represent decreasing return to scale

12.2. Difference between Law of variable proportion and Return to Scale

The distinguish feature between law of variable proportion and return to scale are shown below:

S. No.	Law of variable proportion	Return to scale
01.	Describe the behaviour of output when some factor of production are constant.	Examine the behaviour of one input is varied, when all input are varied at the same time
02.	It is short-run production function	It is long-run production function.
03.	The proportion among factor varies	The proportion among factor remain the same
04.	Here increasing, constant and decreasing return to factor are observed	Here increasing, constant and decreasing return to scale are observed
05.	The diminishing return are due to over exploitation of fixed factor	The Diminishing return to scale are due to operation of diseconomies of scale
06.	$Y=f(X_1 \mid X_2, X_3, \ldots\ldots X_n)$	$Y=f(X_1, X_2, X_3, \ldots\ldots X_n)$
07	It is a reality	It is a myth

13

Cost

13.1. Introduction

Knowledge regarding various relationships existing between costs and output is necessary to comprehend the concepts of equilibrium conditions of different firms under different market conditions. Basically we require data on output, fixed costs, variable costs and the prices of inputs and outputs. From this data we finally derive all the seven cost concepts, *viz.,*TFC, TVC, TC, AFC, AVC, AC and MC. These cost concepts would have implications for output expansion of the firms and equilibrium position of the firms in different time periods. In the cost theory, economists use different names for cost concepts under different context. They are money costs or nominal costs, real costs, opportunity costs, economic costs, implicit costs, explicit costs, deflated costs, social costs, short run costs, long run costs, separable costs, *etc.*

Nominal Costs or Money Costs

These are usually expressed in money terms at current prices. Nominal costs of production refer to per unit cost of production of output at current market prices.

Real Costs

When the costs of inputs and input services are expressed at constant prices they become real costs.

Opportunity Cost

Opportunity cost is the value of return sacrificed or foregone from the next best alternative activity. In farming farmers don't have to pay for their owned resources, *viz.,*family labour, owned bullock labour, owned machinery, owned seed, *etc.* But still in the cost analysis the value of these owned resources are considered on the basis of opportunity cost.

Economic Costs

These are divided into explicit cost and implicit costs. Explicit costs include payments made by the entrepreneurs for purchasing and hiring of inputs and input services. They are also called paid out costs or cash costs. Entrepreneurs do not pay for the use of owned resources. The value of such resources is called as implicit costs. Costs of self – owned and self – employed resources are known as implicit costs.

Deflated Costs

Costs if deflated by general price index are called deflated costs. By doing so the effect of inflation in an economy is taken out. Example: Real cost of commodities.

Social Costs

These are also called as externalities. Firms incur both implicit and explicit costs in the production of goods and services. Their sum constitutes total cost of production. These costs we name as private costs, but from the point of view of society, these firms will give rise to some additional costs to the society in the form of environmental degradation, water, air or noise pollution *etc.*, in the areas where goods are produced by the private firms. In the absence of well – drained system, irrigation projects bring problems to the command area of the project in the form of new diseases. Such costs are called social costs.

Separable Costs

Separable costs are the costs which can exclusively be attributed to production of output separately. Common costs are those which cannot be separated to the production of the output. So they are called joint costs. The costs are involved in the production of several products. For *example,* electricity generation, ground water use, *etc.*

Historical Costs and Replacement Costs

Historical costs are the costs involved in the purchase of durable goods like land, buildings, machinery, equipment, etc. Purchase price of the asset should be considered as price of the asset and hence it is considered as historical cost in analysis. Since the costs of the assets are apportioned in computation, they are called as historical costs. Replacement costs refer to the difference between the purchase price of the asset and the current price of the same asset. Suppose a tractor is purchased 10 years ago at a price of Rs. 1,50,000 but its present price is say, Rs. 2,50,000, the difference of Rs. 1,00,000 is the replacement cost.

Establishment Costs

Construction of plant in any business activity entails some costs. Such construction costs are called establishment costs in the business analysis. They are also called first phase costs. The other costs *viz.,* licenses, site development expenditure for construction of factory, purchase of equipment, furniture, expenditure on personnel, royalties for seeking product rights, cost of raising finance, costs of maintaining raw materials *etc.,* are also included in the establishment costs.

13.2. Cost Concepts

Knowledge regarding the cost functions is very much essential for optimal managerial decisions to be taken by the firm as well as the Government. In the short run, pricing and output decisions are based on short run cost curves, while in the long run, long run cost curves have crucial implications for development and growth of the firm and investment policies of the firm. Consideration of cost curves is essential and forms the basis for entry and exit of the firms in the industry. Profit maximizing rule is determined with the help of cost curves, cost functions and production functions. This rule is popularly known as marginal analysis at which MC = MR. The costs are also one of the major price determinants in all the market situations of the economy and in all the economic models which would explain the behavior of the firms.

There are seven costs, which explain the behavior of the firms in the production of requisite products.

13.2.1. Fixed Costs

Fixed costs remain the same irrespective of level of production. These costs remain invariant in the short run but in the long run there are no fixed costs as all the inputs can be varied. Fixed costs include cost items like taxes, insurance, cess, depreciation on machinery, implements, tools, buildings, salaries of personnel working in the firm, *etc.* These are also known as indirect costs, sunk costs and overhead costs. The summation of all these costs is called total fixed costs (TFC). TFC is a horizontal straight line parallel to X – axis.

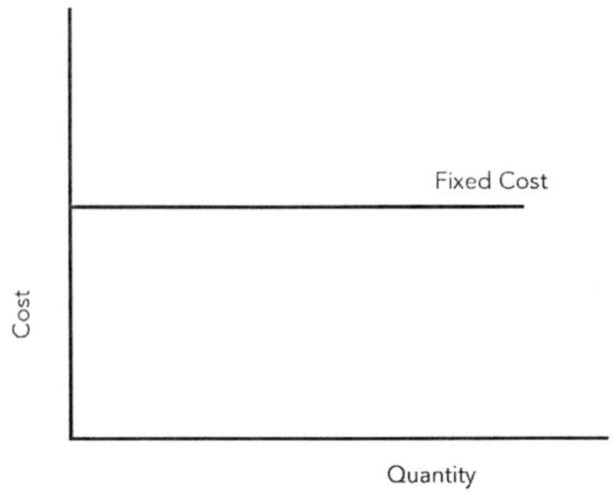

13.2.2. Variable Costs

Variable costs as per definition vary with the level of output. These include costs of raw materials, labour, power, repairs, maintenance charges of machinery, *etc.* These are also known as working costs, operating costs, direct costs, prime costs, circulating costs and running costs. These are second phase costs. The summation of these costs refer to total variable costs (TVC). Graphically TVC as inverse 'S' shape.

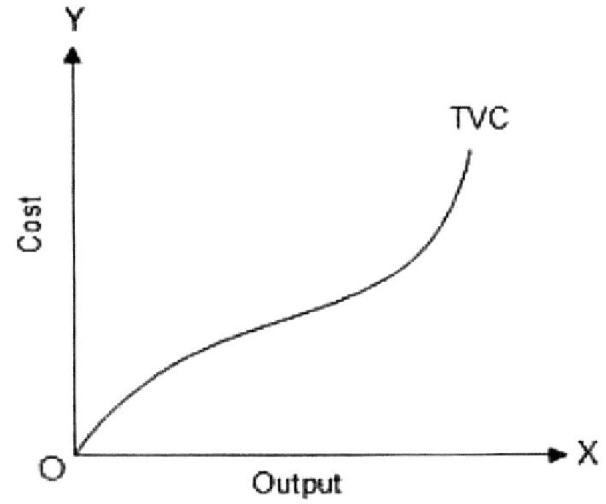

13.2.3 Total Costs

These include total fixed costs as well as total variable costs. Its shape is similar to that of TVC.

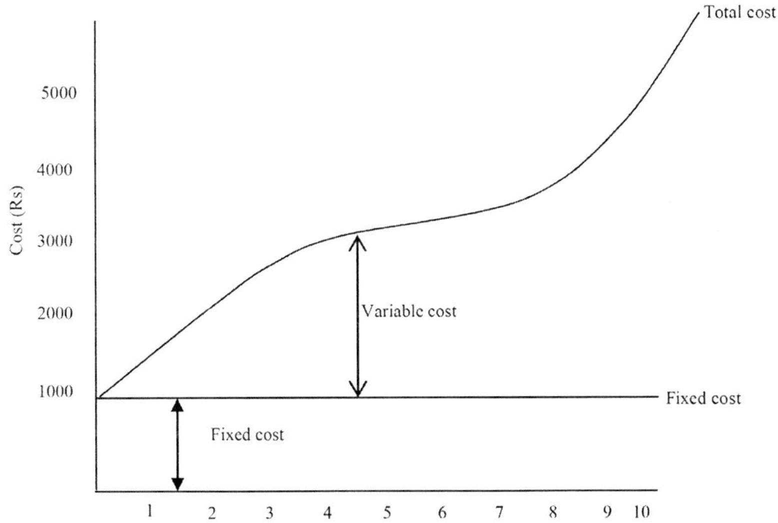

13.2.4. Average Variable Cost (AVC)

It is the amount spent on the variable inputs to produce an unit of output. Algebraically it is expressed as

$$AVC = \frac{Total\,Variable\,cost}{output} = \frac{TVC}{Q}$$

When a small amount of output is produced, cost of variable input per unit of output becomes very high. This is to say in other words, that productivity of variable input increases when greater amounts are used in the production of the commodities due to economies of scale. This causes AVC to have 'U' shape when it is graphed. When it is 'U' shaped it becomes reciprocal of average physical product curve. AVC falls to minimum level at the output level where APP is maximum. Thereafter due to production of greater amount of output, AVC rises again and becomes vertical at certain level of maximum output.

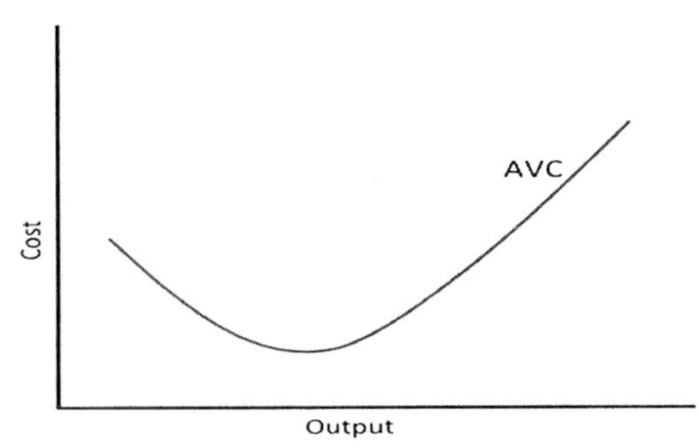

13.2.5 Average Fixed Cost (AFC)

It is the cost of fixed resources or inputs required for producing one unit of output and it is given by the formula as

$$AFC = \frac{Total\ Fixed\ cost}{output} = \frac{TFC}{Q}$$

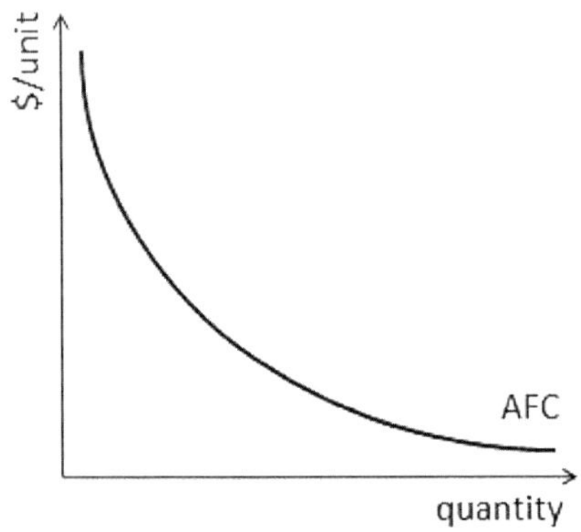

AFC curve is declining with the increased output because TFC is constant. Due to this it is continuously falling up to its maximum output. It is having the shape of hyperbola.

13.2.6. Average Total Cost or Average Cost (ATC or AC)

When the total costs are divided by output, we get ATC.

$$ATC = \frac{Total\ cost}{output} = \frac{TC}{Q} = \frac{TFC + TVC}{Q}$$

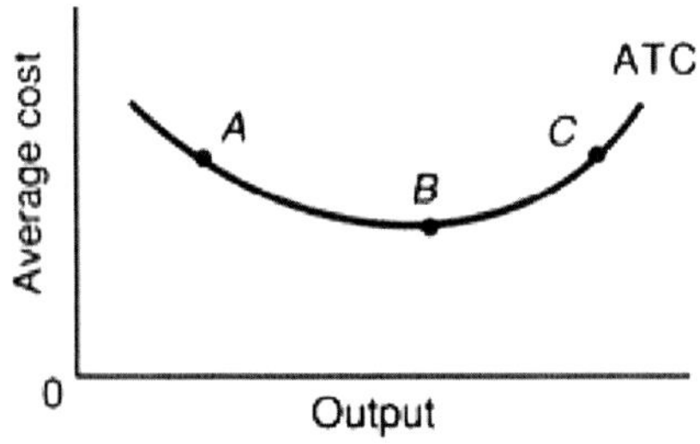

13.2.7 Marginal Cost (MC)

As per the definition, it is the change in the total cost due to the change in output. Algebraically it is expressed as

$$MC = \frac{Change\ in\ total\ cost}{Change\ in\ output} = \frac{\Delta TVC}{\Delta Q}$$

To compute MC, we can use TC or TVC because fixed costs cannot be changed. The only component of change in TC is TVC. The specific shape of MC curve is due to marginal product of the variable inputs. When MPP is maximum, MC is minimum. MC curve is declining when MPP curve is increasing; hence there is an inverse relationship between MPP and MC. When MPP is zero, MC becomes vertical. MC curve intersects AVC and ATC at their minimum points.

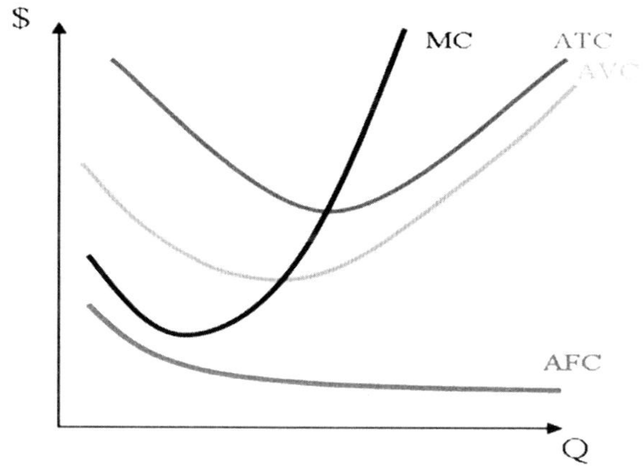

13.3. Short Run and Long Run Costs

In the short run it is possible to vary the output by varying only the amount of variable factors such as labour and raw materials. In the short run, the fixed factors such as capital equipment, managerial persons, factory building etc cannot be changed. Thus in the short run if an organization intends to increase production, then it can be done by hiring more workers or buying and using more raw materials. In the short run it is not possible to enlarge the size of the plant. Thus in the short run only variable factors can be varied and the fixed factors remain the same.

In long run time period it is possible to vary all factors of production. Thus it is possible to increase output in long run either by increasing capital equipment or by adding capacity to existing plant or installing an altogether new plant of bigger size.

13.3.1. Short Run Cost

The short run cost is explained by following hypothetical example.

Table 13.3.1: The short run total cost schedule

Capital Units (Fixed Factor)	Labour Units (Variable factor)	Total product (TP)	Total fixed cost (TFC) (Rs.)	Total Variable cost (TVC)(Rs.)	Total Cost (TC) (TFC + TVC)
5	0	0	150	-	150
5	1	4	150	12	162
5	2	7	150	24	174
5	3	12	150	36	186
5	4	17	150	48	198
5	5	20	150	60	210
5	6	22	150	72	222
5	7	23	150	84	234

The data in the above table shows the behaviour of total fixed cost, total variable cost, total cost in the short run. Following assumptions are made about the data: price of labour is Rs. 12 per Unit and Price of capital is Rs 30 per Unit.

13.3.1.1. Short Run Total Cost

1. Total fixed cost remains same at Rs. 150 at all levels of output. Even when production is not done (TP = 0), total fixed cost is Rs. 150.
2. Total variable costs varies with the output. When production is not done, total variable cost is zero.
3. Total cost varies directly as total variable cost. In the short run fixed cost remains same and change in total cost are affected due to change in variable costs.

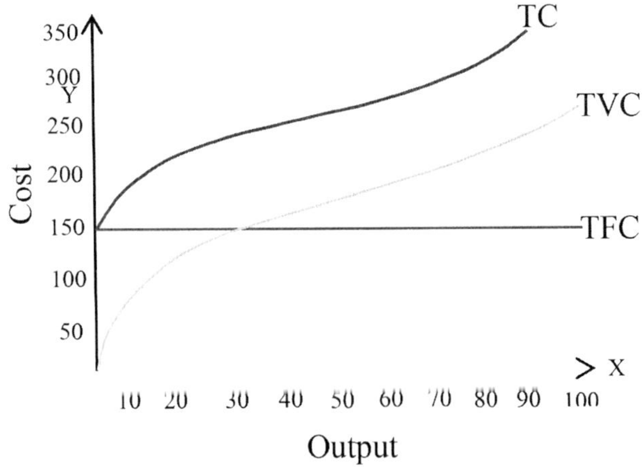

Fig. 13.3.1.1: Total cost, Total variable cost and Fixed cost

13.3.1.2. Short Run Average Cost Curves

For a hypothetical example, average cost curves are shown in the following table.

Table 13.3.1.2: Average cost

Output (Units)	Total Fixed cost (TFC) (Rs.)	Total Variable (TVC) (Rs.)	Total Cost (Rs.)	Average Fixed cost AFC = $\frac{TFC}{Q}$	Average Variable Cost AVC = $\frac{TVC}{Q}$	Average Total Cost ATC = $\frac{TC}{Q}$	Marginal Cost
0	220	0	220	-	-	-	-
1	220	100	320	220	100	320	100
2	220	140	360	110	70	180	40
3	220	160	380	73.33	53.33	126.66	20
4	220	192	412	55	48	103	32
5	220	260	480	44	52	96	68
6	220	400	620	36.66	66.66	103.33	140

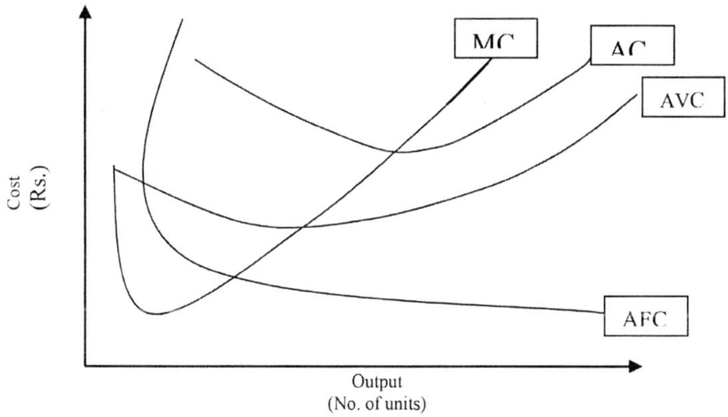

Fig. 13.3.1.2: Average cost

From the above figure, following conclusions can be drawn about short run cost curve:

1. As output increases, average fixed cost decreases. The total fixed cost remains same for all level of output, but average fixed cost decreases continuously because of spreading it over more number of units as output increases.
2. Average variable cost first decreases and then increase as output increases.

3. Average total cost decreases initially. It rcmains same at a point for a while and then go on increasing as output increases.
4. Marginal cost decreases initially but then increases as the output is increased.
5. When the average cost is minimum, marginal cost is equal to average cost.

13.3.2. Long Run Cost Curves

In the long run, all factor inputs are variable, allowing an organization to adjust its overall plant capacity in response to demand. Unlike the short run, where costs are categorized as fixed or variable, the long run considers only variable or direct costs as part of total cost. It serves as a future-oriented planning horizon, but in practice, all economic activities take place in the short run. The long run is essentially a collection of multiple short-run scenarios, from which businesses select the most suitable operational strategy. The long-run average cost (LRAC) curve, therefore, acts as an **envelope** for various short-run cost curves, as it is drawn tangent to them. This concept is illustrated through a cost curve based on three possible plant sizes.

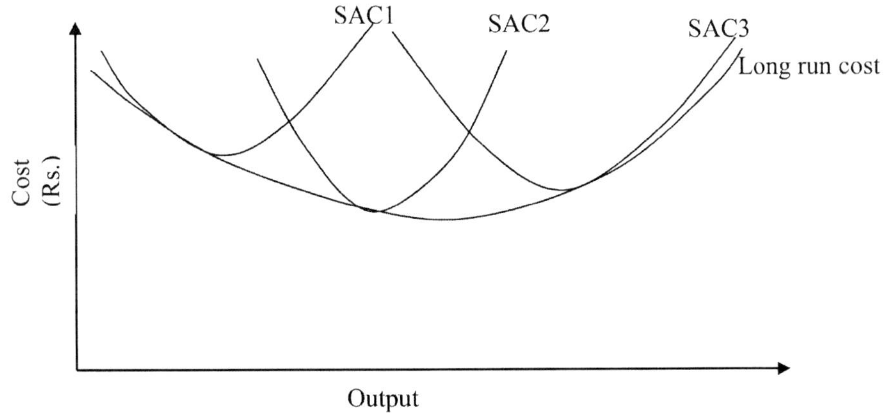

Fig. 13.3.2: Long run cost

14

Supply

14.1. Meaning

Supply in agriculture refers to the availability of agricultural products, both raw and processed, for distribution to markets, consumers, or other industries. This includes crops, livestock, dairy products, fruits, vegetables, and other agricultural goods. "*Supply is the amount of a commodity that sellers are able and willing to offer for sale at different price per unit of time*".

In the words of *Meyer* "Supply is a schedule of the amount of a good that would be offered for sale at all possible price at any period of time; e.g., a day, a week, and so on".

14.2. Stock

Stock in agriculture refers to the quantity of inputs and resources available for farming, such as seeds, fertilizers, pesticides, machinery, and livestock. It encompasses all the assets and materials that a farmer or agricultural operation has on hand to support the production process.

"***Stock*** is meant the total quantity of a commodity this exists in a market and can be offered for sale at a short notice".

14.3. Stocks Vs Supply

- Supply may be defined as the active stock (actual quantity) which is made available for the consumers at the prevailing market prices.
- Supply is flow concept.
- Stock is the quantity of different commodities which are stored; they are made available to the consumer when there are favourable prices.

14.4. Law of Supply

As per law of supply, there is direct relationship between the price of a commodity and its quantity offered for sale over a specified period of time. When the price of a goods rises, other things remaining the same, its quantity offered for sale increases and vice versa. This relationship between price and the quantities which suppliers are prepared to offer for sale is called the *law of supply*.

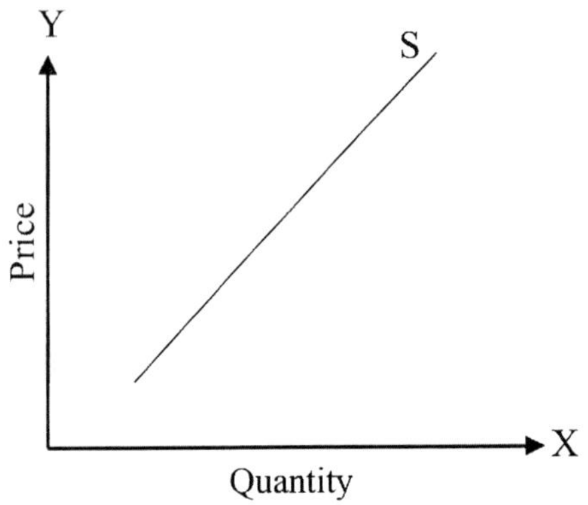

Explanation of Law of Supply

The *law of supply*, in short, states that ceteris paribus sellers supply more goods at a higher price than they are willing at a lower price.

14.5. Supply Function

The supply function is now explained with the help of a schedule and a curve.

$Qs = f\ (Px\ Tech,\ S_i\ F_n,\ X, ...)$

Where,

Qs = Quantity supplied of commodity,

P_x = Price of commodity,

Tech = Technology,

S = Supplies of inputs,

F = Features of nature &

X = Taxes/Subsidies.

14.6 Supply Schedule

It is a statement in the form of a table that shows the different quantities of a commodity that a firm or a producer offers for sale in the market at different prices.

It denotes the relationship between the supply and the price, while all non-price variables remain constant. There are two types of Supply Schedules: i) Individual Supply schedule and ii) Market supply schedule

14.6.1. Individual Supply schedule

It is a supply schedule that depicts the supply by an individual firm or producer of a commodity in relation to its price. Let us understand it with the help of an example.

Price per unit of commodity X (Px)	Quantity supplied of commodity X (Sx)
300	30
325	40
350	50
375	60
400	70

The above schedule depicts the individual supply schedule. We can see that when the price of the commodity is ₹100, its supply is 1000 units. Similarly, when its price is ₹500, its supply increases to 5000 units.

Thus, we can conclude that as the price falls the supply decreases and as the price rises the supply also increases. Hence, there exists a direct relationship between the price and quantity supplied.

Individual Supply Curve

It is a graphical representation of the individual supply schedule. The X-axis represents the supply and Y-axis represents the price of a commodity. There exists a direct relationship between price and quantity supplied of a commodity. The individual supply curve is drawn based on first and last column of the table.

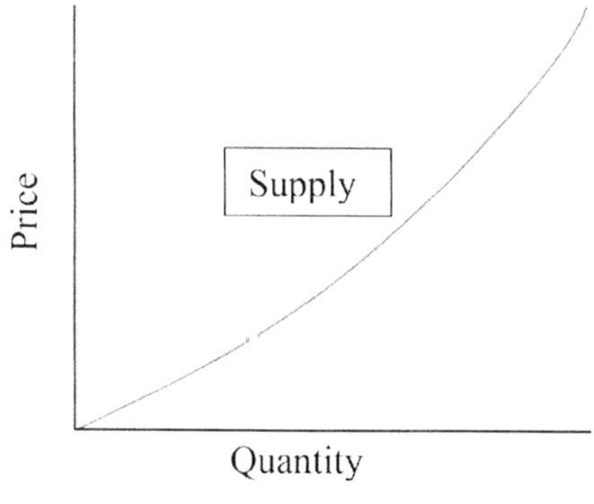

14.6.2. Market Supply Schedule

It is a summation of the individual supply schedules and depicts the supply of different customers for a commodity in relation to its price. Let us understand it with the help of an example.

Price per unit of commodity X (Px)	Quantity supplied by firm A (Q_A)	Quantity supplied by firm B (Q_B)	Market Supply (Q_A+Q_B)
100	1000	3000	4000
200	2000	4000	6000
300	3000	5000	8000
400	4000	6000	10000
500	5000	7000	12000

The above schedule shows the market supply of commodity X. When the price of the commodity is ₹100, firm A supplies 1000 units while the firm B supplies 3000 units.

Thus, the market supply is 4000 units. Similarly, when its price is ₹500, firm A supplies 5000 units while firm B supplies 7000 units. Thus, it's market demand increases to 12000 units.

Thus, we can conclude that whether it is the individual supply or the market supply, the law **of supply governs both of them.**

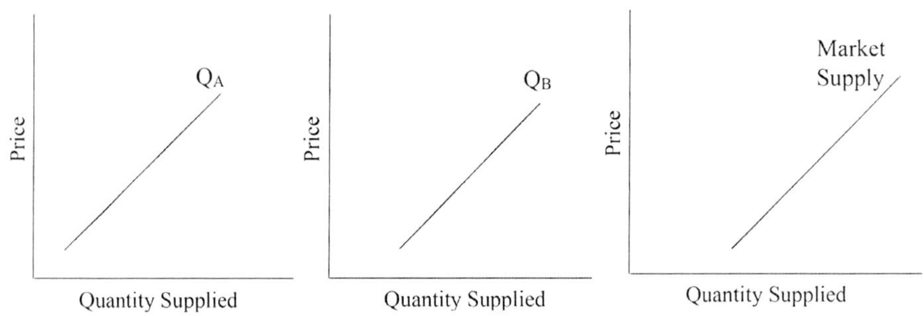

Market Supply Curve

It is a graphical representation of the market supply schedule. The X-axis represents the market supply in units and Y-axis represents the price of a commodity. The market supply curve is drawn based on first and last column of the table.

14.6.3. Shift in supply curve and Movement along Supply curve

- Movement along Supply curve or Extension and Contraction in supply extension and contraction in supply follows the law of supply. Extension in supply means an increase in quantity sold due to increase in prices of the commodity under consideration (keeping all other factors are constant). Contraction in supply means an decrease in quantity sold due to decrease in prices of the commodity under consideration (keeping all other factors are constant).

- A shift in the supply curve or Increase and decrease in supply refers to the change in supply not due to change in price but due to change in the values of other variables influencing supply.
- Increase in supply means more supply at the same price and decrease in supply means less supply at the same price.

14.7 Determinants of Supply

There are four important Determinants of Supply given as under:

1. **Technology changes.** Technology helps a producer to minimize his cost of production.
2. **Resource supplies.** The producer also has to pay for other resources such as raw materials and labour. if his money is short on supplying a certain number of products because of an increase in resource supplies, then he has to reduce his supply.
3. **Tax/ Subsidy.** A producer aims to maximize his profit, but an increase in tax will only increase his expenses, decreasing his capacity to buy resource supplies and forcing him to reduce his supply.
4. **Price of other goods produced.** A producer may not only produce one product but other products as well. A producer's money is limited and if he increases his supply in one product, he would have to decrease his supply in the other product, no unless his sales increase.

   Where, $Q_x^s = f(P_x)$ Ceteris Paribus

14.8. Elasticity of supply

Elasticity of supply is an economic concept that assesses the responsiveness of the quantity supplied of a good or service to changes in its price. In simple terms, it measures the extent to which producers or suppliers can adjust their production or market offerings in response to price fluctuations. This responsiveness is typically quantified using the following formula:

$$\text{Elasticity of Supply (Es)} = \frac{\text{\% Change in Quantity Supplied}}{\text{\% Change in Price}}$$

14.8.1. Degree of elasticity of Supply

There are five degree of elasticity of supply. They are follows:

01. **Perfectly Elastic Supply** (Es $= \infty$): In this extreme case, a small change in price leads to an infinitely large change in quantity supplied. Producers can adjust production instantly, so the supply is perfectly responsive to price changes.

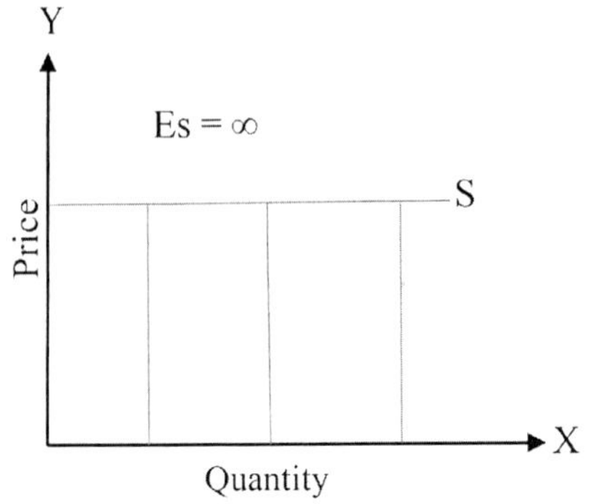

02. Relatively Elastic Supply (Es > 1): When elasticity of supply is greater than 1, it means that a percentage change in price results in a more than proportionate percentage change in the quantity supplied. Producers can adjust their production, but not instantaneously.

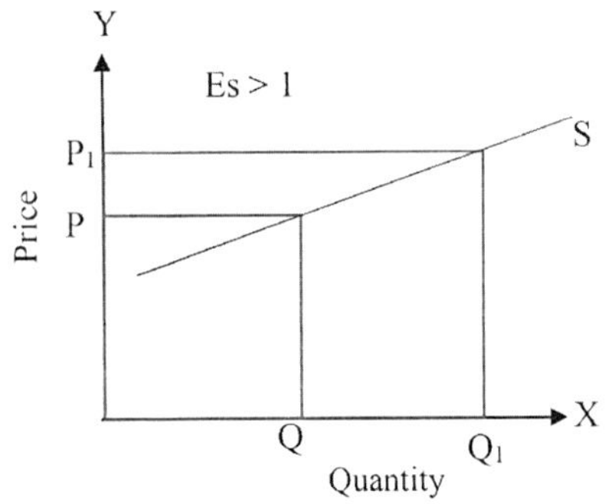

03. Unitary Elastic Supply (Es = 1): When the elasticity of supply equals 1, it means that the percentage change in quantity supplied is exactly proportional to the percentage change in price. Producers can adjust production in line with price changes.

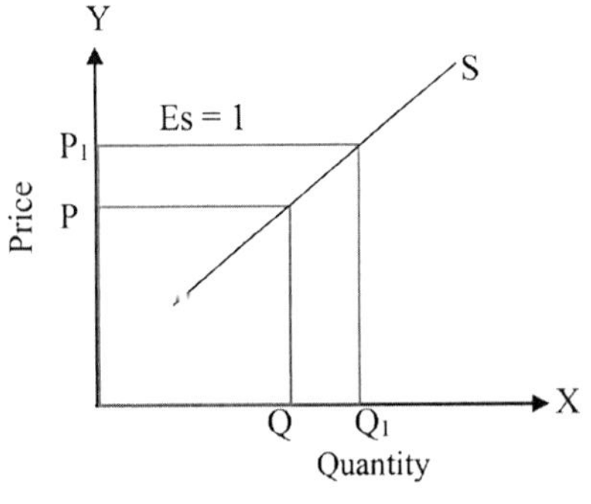

04. Relatively Inelastic Supply (Es < 1): In this case, the elasticity of supply is less than 1, indicating that a percentage change in price leads to a less than proportionate percentage change in the quantity supplied. Producers cannot easily adjust their production in response to price fluctuations.

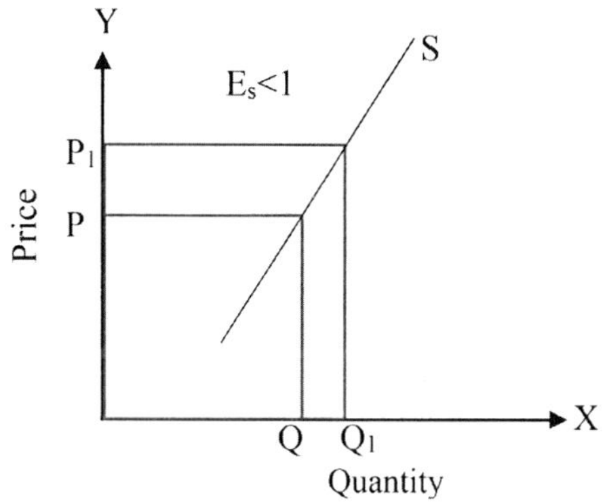

05. Perfectly Inelastic Supply (Es = 0): This is the extreme opposite of perfectly elastic supply. In this case, the quantity supplied remains constant regardless of price changes. Producers are unable to adjust production in response to price variations.

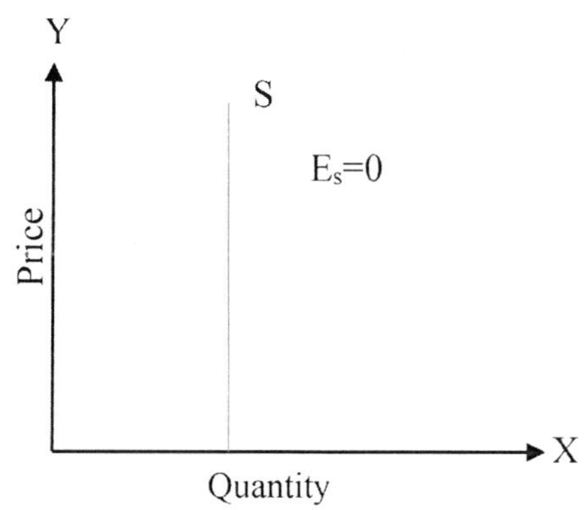

14.9. Market Equilibrium: A market can be said in equilibrium if it follows the following conditions

- Quantity Demanded is equal to Quantity Supplied
- At the point where both demand and supply curve intersects.

Market Inequilibrium Conditions: A market is said to be in in equilibrium if it follows the following conditions

- Quantity Demanded is greater than Quantity Supplied (condition of Shortage)
- Quantity Demanded is less than Quantity Supplied (Condition of Surplus).

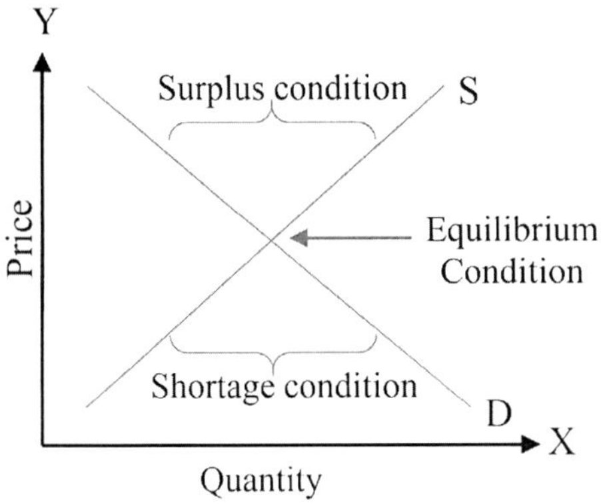

15

Distribution

15.1. Meaning

While doing production of goods, the producer coordinates different factors of production *i.e.,* land, labour, capital and management. In the process of distribution the returns obtained through the production activity are apportioned to these factors that are employed in the production process. Consequently land gets rent, labour gets wages and interest is paid to capital and finally organization is rewarded with profit. Such an apportionment of returns among different factors of production is called distribution. It is also called factor pricing.

15.1.2. Rent

Rent is the return for the fertility status of the land. In fact the land is defined in a broad sense. All the natural resources existing on the surface and beneath the surface of land like mines, rivers, *etc.,* are also treated as land, from which rent is received. Some resources are publicly owned, while others are privately owned. Rent is almost zero for publicly owned resource because one cannot use it for one's own purpose. These are meant for public welfare. Rent is expressed in two forms *i.e.,* one is economic rent and the other is contract rent.

15.1.3. Economic Rent

Economic rent is the rent received exclusively from the use of land only. We use the term, exclusively because the rent of a building referred as the return obtained by the owner on the capital invested in the construction of building as well as the land. It is the return obtained from the combined values of both. In that case, it no longer qualifies as rent. In farming the rent paid by a tenant to the landlord is not economic rent.

15.1.4. Contract Rent

This implies the money paid by the tenant to the land lord for cultivating the land in a given year. Normally a certain rent is charged by a farmer not only for land but also for making availability of certain infrastructure on land like buildings, machinery, wells, fencing, *etc.* This means that he would like to realize some return on the investment made on the farm. Then it is not exclusively rent for land only. Thus economic rent is a part of contract rent.

15.1.5. Quasi Rent

The basis for evolving this rent is the short run fixity of man made assets of production like machines, buildings, *etc.* When in the short run, the demand for these assets increases, consequently their income also increases. This results in a surplus income due to increased demand. This surplus income of assets is called quasi rent This rise in quasi rent is a temporary phenomenon. In fact, the supply of these assets being elastic it is increased in the long run to match with the demand causing the surplus earnings to disappear. The concept of quasi rent does not apply to land because supply of land is inelastic.

15.1.6. Scarcity Rent

This is the rent which arises due to scarcity of land in relation to demand. Scarcity rent is due to inelastic supply of land. This is surplus rent over the market rent for land due to increased demand for land.

15.2. Modern Theory of Rent

Modern economists assert that rent arises for any factor of production. It is the surplus payment in excess of transfer earnings of a factor. Transfer earnings imply the amount of money which any particular unit of factor could earn in its next best alternative use.

The rent of the land is determined by the two market forces *viz.,* demand for and supply of land. Demand curve for land slopes downwards because the rent of land is influenced by the marginal productivity. On the other hand supply of land is fixed *i.e.,* supply is inelastic. Supply curve is vertical to X – axis. Equilibrium between demand and supply determines the rent of land.

As seen from figure, D_2 is the demand curve for land and S is the supply curve of land. The two curves intersect at 'E_2' and hence the rent is OR_2. Changes in population and consequent additional pressure on land increase the demand for land. Therefore the new demand curve is D_3 and the rent is OR_3. Contrary to this when demand for land falls the new demand curve D_1 is formed and its corresponding rent is OR_1.

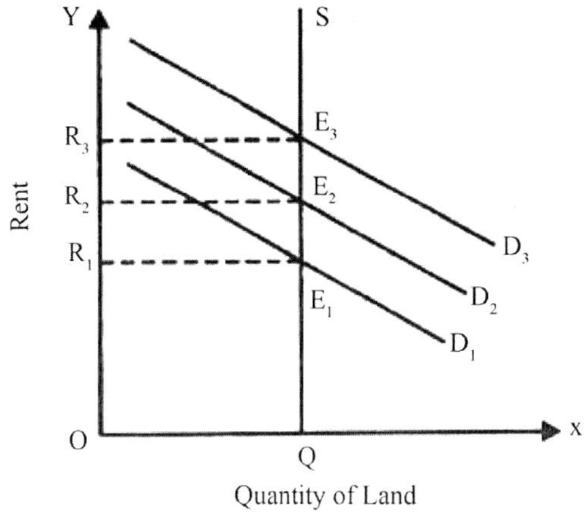

15.3. Wages

Wages are the rewards paid for the labourers for sparing their productive services. It may be paid either in cash or kind or both. *A wage may be defined as a sum of money paid under contract by an employer to a worker for services rendered (Benham).* Wages are paid for casual labourers, while salaries are paid for permanent staff and consultation fee for doctors, lawyers, etc.

15.3.1. Methods of Wage Payment

Based on the payment, wages are classified as (1) Cash wages and kind wages (2) Time wages (3) Piece wages; and (4) Task wages.

1. **Cash Wages and Kind Wages:** Wages for the workers are paid in cash or kind or both. With the advent of currency, wages are paid in cash. However, kind payment is also in vogue along with the cash payment.
2. **Time Wages:** It is the wage per unit of time. It is the payment of wages on hourly, daily, weekly, fortnightly and monthly basis. In farming, casual labourers are paid on daily basis, workers for domestic services are paid on monthly basis and attached servants in farming are paid on half – yearly or yearly basis.
3. **Piece Wages:** It is based on the work performed by an individual in the production of goods and services. In the manufacturing process of a good, the entire production activity is divided into various sub – processes. An individual attending to a sub – process is paid according to the work he completes on a particular day.
4. **Task Wages:** Wages are paid for a given work after its completion, say in farming, paddy transplanting, weeding, harvesting, *etc.,* are completed

by a group of labourers. Wages are decided based on the work assigned to the group and it has nothing to do with the number of labourers in that group. The task is given to the group for completion of work in time according to agreed wages. They are also called as contract wages.

15.3.2. Types of Wages

1. **Nominal Wage or Money Wage:** It is the wage paid in terms of money at current market prices.
2. **Real Wage:** It indicates the purchasing power of money wage. Real wage of the worker is obtained by dividing nominal wage of the workers at different time periods by general price index. Real wage is measured by

   $R = W/P$

   Where,

   R = Real wage

   W = Money wage

   P = General price index

15.3.3. Modern Theory

Modern theory is based on demand for and supply of labour. Demand for labour is a derived demand. If there is a higher demand for products from consumers, there would be more demand from producers for labour for helping to bring the expected level of output.

A rise in demand for a commodity pushes up the demand for the labour involved in the production of that commodity.

The supply of labour is represented by the number of workers willing to work in a production activity at various wage rates taking into consideration the number of hours, number of days in a week, *etc.* These two forces *i.e.,* demand and supply determine the wages.

DD is the demand for labour and SS is the supply of labour. The wage rate is OW.

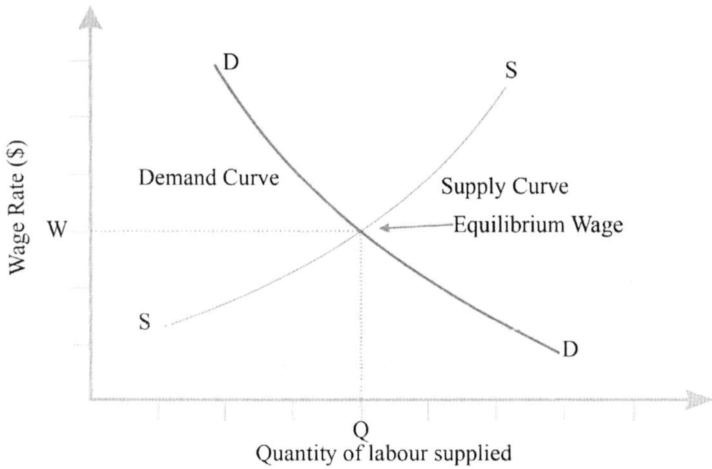

Equilibrium Level of Employment

15.4. Interest

Interest is the amount paid by the borrower to the lender for the use of capital. According to Marshall *"the payment made by a borrower for the use of loan for, say a year, is expressed as the ratio which that payment bears to the loan"* is called interest.

Interest is the price paid for the use of loanable funds (Meyers).

The interest charged by a lender from the borrower is termed as gross interest. It is because lending activity is fraught with risk as well as inconvenience which are also considered. Taking these items into account the gross interest is considered under the following terms.

1. **Net or Pure Interest:** This interest is the payment exclusively made for the loan amount.
2. **Insurance Against Risk:** In the lending activity there is always the risk of not getting back the funds lent by the lender. The loan may turn out into a bad debt. This risk needs to be insured. For this purpose, some more interest is added to the net interest.
3. **Payment for Inconvenience:** Through the lending activity the lender gets interest but in the same process he is placed in inconveniencc to get back his funds at the time he wants, because the funds are locked up for a certain period of time. Unless the loan period was over he cannot get back his funds. For this inconvenience, he charges some additional interest to the net interest.

4. **Reward for Management:** The business of lending requires perfect maintenance of the records to keep a close watch on the business performance. Apart from this, the borrowers are to be pursued for prompt repayment. This calls for efficient management of the business. Hence reward for management is included in gross interest.

15.4.1. Determination of Interest Rate

Liquidity preference and supply of money determine the rate of interest. Liquidity preference here means the liquidity preference for speculative purpose according to Keynes. Therefore, the equilibrium between liquidity preference for speculative purpose and supply of money determine the rate of interest.

In figure, LP indicates liquidity preference for speculative purpose. It is the demand for money. OQ represents the fixed amount of money available to meet the requirements of liquidity preference for speculative purpose. Rate of interest is determined by the equality of demand of money for speculative purpose and supply of money. The interest rate that prevails is OR, which is the equilibrium interest.

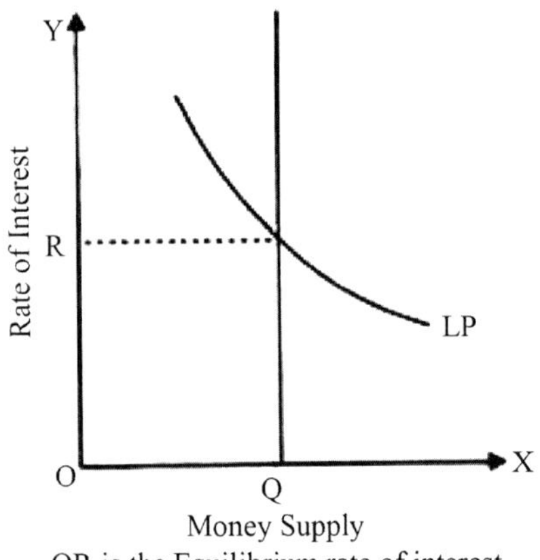

OR is the Equilibrium rate of interest

15.5. Profit

Profit is the reward for entrepreneurial function of decision – making and uncertainty bearing. Profit can be either positive or negative, since it is a residual income. Profit differs from rewards of other factors of production like rent, wages and interest on the point that these are all certain, while profit is tentative. These rewards are paid even before the ultimate product is obtained, while profit happens to be the surplus of returns over total costs, and it is obtained at the end of production activity.

15.3.1. Various Concepts of Profit

Gross Profit: It is the surplus of gross revenue over paid out costs (explicit costs) obtained in a production activity. Gross profit cannot be treated as ultimate profit, for it includes several items which are not actually profits as presented below:

Remuneration for Entrepreneur Himself: It is a practice for the entrepreneur to contribute his own capital in the business besides offering his services as a manager. In such a situation the opportunity cost of owned capital and the services rendered in his own business are also included in the gross profit. These imputed costs are to be deducted from the gross profit to arrive at the net profit.

Depreciation and Maintenance Charges: When the plant is in operation there will be wear and tear (depreciation) on equipment and machinery which needs to be duly accounted for. In addition to this, interest on fixed capital and insurance premium are other fixed cost items that are incurred in a production activity. These cost items need to be deducted from the gross profit to arrive at net profit.

Extra Personal Profits: These are the profits which accrue to a business unit not due to the managerial ability of the entrepreneur, but due to other factor, say the profits of monopoly. These are not due to the businessman's managerial abilities but for his position as a monopolist. The monopoly profit needs to be deducted from gross profit to arrive at net profit. Another source of getting unexpected high profit is from windfall gains or chance profits. Any sudden happening, say outbreak of war, natural calamities in certain pockets of the country etc., lead to a rise in the product prices, resulting in abnormal profits for the entrepreneur. Such unexpected profits should be deducted from gross profit to find out the net profit.

Net Profit: The aforesaid three items viz., remuneration for entrepreneur himself, depreciation and maintenance charges and extra personal profits are to be deducted from gross profit to work out the net profit. It is the reward of the entrepreneur for coordination and risk – taking.

Net profit = Gross income – Total cost

16

National Income

16.1. Meaning

National Income is nothing but the aggregate money value of all goods and services produced in a country in a year. It can also be viewed as income distributed among the factors of production in the form of rent (to land), wages (to labour) interest (to capital) and profits (to entrepreneurs).

According to Alfred Marshal National Income is defined as the labour and capital of a country acting on its natural resources produce annually a certain net aggregate of goods and services.

16.1.1. Limitations

- In an economy in which numerous goods and services are produced, it is really a difficult proposition to estimate them correctly to arrive at the national income. Coming to the farming, farmers do retain some part of production for personal consumption and the rest is only marketed. In such a case, the methodology to evaluate the amount of produce not reached the market has not been given.
- Double counting: It implies the same good being counted twice: say, cotton may be counted in agricultural production and the cotton cloth in industrial production.

Marshall approached national income from **production end**. On the other hand, some other economist approached from **consumption end**. At the same time this approach in reality poses problems. Consumers who number in millions, consumes the same good at different places, and the estimation of their total consumption is a difficult proposition. Hence, there are problems in measurement of national income.

16.1.2. Modern View

Simon Kuznets defined national income as **"the net output of goods and services flowing during the year from the production to the hands of ultimate consumers"**. Here the income side as well as expenditure side is included to present the concept of national income.

16.1.3. Gross National Product (GNP)

GNP is the basic social accounting measure of the total production of goods and services in an economy. **GNP is defined as the total market value of all final goods and services produced in a year.** It includes the market value of such products as are produced in agriculture, mines, forests, industries etc. and of services like transport, communication, banks, lawyers, doctors, teachers, etc. and these are added together during one year.

GNP is a measure of current output of economic activity in a country. Goods and services produced in an economy are subjected to purchase and sale several times. Therefore, to avoid the possibilities of double counting, GNP includes the market value of **final goods only** ignoring the transactions involving intermediate goods.

Those which are not included in GNP are as follows

1. Services which are rendered freely e.g. free services offered by family members to others in the family.
2. The sale and purchase of old goods (resale of used items).
3. The sale and purchase of shares, bonds, etc... because they do not add anything to the national produce as they are simply transformed from one to other.
4. Old age pensions, unemployment allowances etc. as they do not provide any services.
5. The change in value of the capital assets as a result of changes in the market prices as they have nothing to do with the current production.

16.2. Measures of GNP

Three methods to measure GNP are as under:

16.2.1. Income Method

According to this method GNP is the sum total of the following items:

a. Wages and salaries
b. Rents
c. Interest
d. Income of Non-company Business (individual proprietors/partners/self-employed person)
e. Corporate profits
f. Indirect taxes

g. Depreciation

h. Transfer payments (payments received by individuals as pension, unemployment allowance are called transfer payments. These are received by the people for not doing any work, so these should be deducted from GNP.

Thus, **GNP = Wages and salaries + Rents + Interest + Incomes of Non-company Business + Corporate profits + Indirect taxes + Depreciation - Transfer payments**

16.2.2. Expenditure Method

Through this, GNP is the sum total of expenditure incurred on goods and services during a period of one year. The expenditures included are as under:

a. **Personal consumption expenditure (C)**: It includes all types of expenditure on personal consumption by individuals of a country. It includes expenses on durable goods (car, bike, tv, mobile, etc.) non-durable goods or consumable articles (food, cloth, soaps, etc.) and also the expenditure incurred on services of all kind (doctor, transportation, etc.)

b. **Gross domestic private investment (I)**: It includes private investment on capital and producer goods like buildings, machinery, equipment's, etc. which are produced in the year only. Purchase of used items and old buildings are not included here because they were included earlier. Investment on purchase of share in stock exchange is also not included, since it does not help in new production.

c. **Net foreign investment (X-M)**: In an economy, the entire production may not be consumed within the country and part of it is exported to other countries. Similarly, the country imports some products from other countries. The difference between the value of exports and of imports should be worked out. If the difference is positive, it should be added to other items of expenditure and it should be deducted from the other items of expenditure, if the difference is negative.

d. **Government expenditure on goods and services (G)**: The Central and State Governments purchase consumer goods as well as investment goods for their own enterprise. Apart from this, the Government spends on defense, police, education, etc. These are included in GNP however, expenditure on transfer payments such as pension, unemployment allowances, etc. are not included in GNP.

   In short, **GNP = C + I + (X-M) + G**

16.2.3. Value added Method

It is always difficult to distinguish between intermediate goods (raw materials, fuel, etc.) and the final goods as it may be intermediate product for one industry and final product for the other industry. For example, electricity is intermediate good when consumed by industry and it is final good when consumed directly by consumers. So, to overcome this problem the value of the intermediate goods used in a manufacturing industry should be deducted from the value of the final goods. The difference that is arrives at is called value addition. If the same procedure is adopted for all the industries in the economy, we can find the GNP by value added method.

National Income at Market Price or Net National Product (NNP)

In the production process, the capital goods are worn-out. This amount of decline in the value of capital goods due to wear and tear is called depreciation. To estimate NNP, depreciation is deducted from GNP. NNP therefore is the market value of all final goods after duly accounting for depreciation; hence, it is called National Income at Market Price. In other words, NNP is the net money value of final goods and services produced at current prices in a year in a country.

Thus, **NNP = GNP – Depreciation**

National Income at Factor Cost : It implies the sum of all incomes earned by resource suppliers for their contribution of land, labour, capital and entrepreneur which go into the net production in a year. In fact national income depicts how much it costs the society in terms of resources to produce net output. Hence, it is called national income at factor cost.

Thus, National Income at Factor Cost = NNP – indirect taxes + subsidies.

GDP vs GNP (or GNI)

Gross Domestic Product (GDP) differs from Gross National Product (GNP) or Gross National Income (GNI) in terms of scope. GDP is based on location, whereas GNP is based on ownership. GDP measures the total production within a country's borders, while GNP accounts for production by enterprises owned by the country's citizens, regardless of location.

If all productive enterprises in a country were owned by its citizens, GDP and GNP would be identical. However, due to foreign ownership, GDP and GNP become non-identical. Production within the country, by a foreign-owned enterprise contributes to its GDP but not its GNP. Conversely, production by a citizen-owned enterprise located abroad is included in GNP but not GDP.

If we take India as an example, the India's GNP is the value of output produced by Indian-owned firms, irrespective of where the firms are located.

Adjustments to GDP (the real, or constant, GDP)

When comparing GDP figures between different years, it is important to adjust for changes in the value of money due to inflation or deflation. The unadjusted or raw GDP is calculated using standard formula which is known as nominal, historical, or current GDP. However, to make comparisons more accurate, this figure can be modified by applying a ratio that accounts for the difference in money value between the measured year and a chosen base year. For instance, if a country's GDP was $100 million in 1990 and $300 million in 2000, but inflation had reduced the currency's value by half, adjusting the 2000 GDP to 1990 terms would require multiplying it by one-half. This results in an adjusted GDP of $150 million in *1990 monetary terms*, revealing that actual economic growth was 1.5 times rather than the apparent threefold increase suggested by the nominal GDP.

The GDP adjusted for changes in money value is referred to as real or constant GDP. The factor used to convert nominal GDP into constant GDP is called the **GDP deflator**. Using constant GDP figures allows for the calculation of the GDP growth rate, which measures the real increase or decrease in a country's production compared to the previous year.

16.2.4. Per Capita GDP

Another factor that may require adjustment is population growth. If a country's GDP doubles over a period while its population triples, the economic growth might not be as significant as it appears. In such a case, the average output per person would decline, suggesting reduced productivity per individual. Per-capita GDP is the metric used to adjust for population growth, offering a clearer picture of economic progress on an individual level.

16.3. The Circular Flow in a Simple Economy

The concept of circular flow is described in its simplest form, a simple economy is considered in which there is no government, no financial markets, and no imports or exports. As an illustration, imagine that the households in this economy live entirely from hand to mouth, spending all their income on consumer goods as soon as they receive it, and that the firms sell all their output directly to consumers as soon as they produce it.

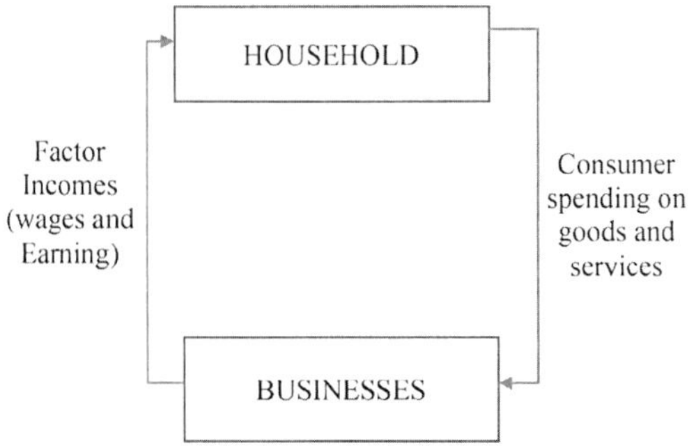

16.4. Methods of Measuring National Income

National income can be measured using four different methods. The choice of method depends on the availability of data in a country and the specific objective being pursued.

(1) **Product Method:** This method involves calculating the total market value of final goods and services produced within a country over a year. To determine GNP, data from all productive sectors—such as agriculture, forestry, mining, industrial production, as well as contributions from transport, communication, insurance, legal services, medical professionals, and educators—are gathered and evaluated at market prices. Only the final goods and services are considered, while intermediate goods and services are excluded.

(2) **Income Method:** This method calculates national income by summing up the net earnings received by all citizens of a country in a given year. It includes net income from all factors of production, such as net rents, wages, interest, and profits. However, income received from transfer of payments are excluded. Income data is collected from various sources, such as tax records for high-income groups and wage bills for workers.

(3) **Expenditure Method:** This method determines national income by summing up the total expenditure made by society in a given year. It includes personal consumption, net domestic investment, government spending on goods and services, and net foreign investment. This approach is based on the assumption that national income is equivalent to national expenditure.

(4) **Value Added Method:** Another approach to measuring national income is by calculating the value added by industries. This is determined by the difference between the value of outputs and inputs at each stage of production. Summing up these differences across all industries in the economy results in the gross domestic product.

16.5. Problems of Measurement of National Income in a Developing Economy

In a developing economy, complete and reliable information relating to the various methods of estimating national income are not available due to the following problems:

1. **Non – monetized sector**: There is a large non – monetized sector in a developing economy. This is the subsistence sector in rural areas in which a large portion of production is partly exchanged for the other goods and is partly kept for personal consumption. Such production and consumption cannot be calculated in national income.
2. **Lack of Occupational Specialization**: There is the lack of occupational specialization in such a country which makes the estimation of national income by product method difficult. Besides the crop, farmers in a developing country are engaged in supplementary occupations like dairying, poultry, cloth making, etc. But income from such productive activities is not included in the national income estimates.
3. **Non – market Transactions**: People living in rural areas in a developing country are able to avoid expenses by building their own huts, tools, implements, garments and other essential commodities. Similarly, people in urban areas having kitchen gardens produce vegetables which they consume themselves. All such productive activities do not enter the market transactions and hence are not included in the national income estimates.
4. **Illiteracy:** The majority of people in developing countries are illiterate and they do not keep any accounts about the production and sales of their products. Under the circumstances, the estimates of production and earned incomes are simply guesses.
5. **Non – availability of Data**: Adequate and correct production and cost data are not available in a developing country. Such data relate to crops, forestry, fisheries, animal husbandry, and the activities of petty shopkeepers, small enterprises, construction workers, etc. For estimating national income by the income method, data on unearned incomes and on persons employed in the service sector are not available. Moreover, data on consumption and investment expenditures of the rural and urban population are not available for the estimation of national income by the expenditure method. Moreover, there is no machinery for the collection of data in such countries.

16.6. Importance of National Income Analysis

The national income data hold the following significance.

1. **For the Economy**: National income data play a crucial role in a country's economy. Today, they are considered the economy's financial records, commonly referred to as social accounts. These accounts represent net national income and net national expenditure, which ultimately balance each other. Social accounts illustrate how a nation's total income, output and production stem from individual earnings, industrial production, and international trade transactions. Their key components are interconnected, allowing each account to be used to verify the accuracy of others.
2. **National policies**: National income data serve as the foundation for national policies, including employment policy. These figures help identify trends in industrial output, investment, and savings, allowing policymakers to implement appropriate measures to steer the economy in the right direction.
3. **Economic Planning**: In today's era of economic planning, national income data hold significant importance. Effective planning requires comprehensive data on a country's gross income, output, savings, and consumption from various sources. Without this information, planning becomes impossible. Likewise, economists develop both short-term and long-term economic and investment models, in which national income data play a crucial role.
4. **Economic Models**: Economists build short – run and long – run economic models in which the national income data are widely used.
5. **For research**: Research scholars in economics also utilize national income data. They analyze various aspects such as a country's input, output, income, savings, consumption, investment, and employment, all of which are derived from social accounts.
6. **Per Capita Income**: National income data play a crucial role in determining a country's per capita income, which indicates its economic well-being. A higher per capita income signifies greater economic welfare, while a lower per capita income suggests the opposite.
7. **Distribution of Income**: National income statistics provide insight into the distribution of income within a country. By analyzing data on wages, rent, interest, and profits, we can identify income disparities among different social groups. Additionally, these statistics reveal the regional distribution of income. Based on this information, the government can

implement policies to reduce income inequality and restore regional balance. Measures such as increasing taxes and expanding public expenditure to address these personal and regional imbalances are also guided by national income statistics.

17

Population

17.1. Theories of Population

The theory of population is studied because the supply of labour depends upon population and its growth. Observing the abnormal growth of population and consequent fall in the standard of living, Thomas Malthus (1760 – 1834) an English Clergyman first studied population growth in various countries of Europe. Later he wrote a book entitled "*An Essay on the Principles of Population*" in 1798. His observations compelled him to foresee a gloomy future for the human race and hence emphasized the immediate need to keep the population growth under check. Now his theory is popularly known as Malthusian theory of population. To quote the theory in his own words "*By nature human food increases in a slow arithmetic ratio, man himself increases in a quick geometric ratio unless want and vice stop him.*"

17.1.2. Propositions of Malthusian Theory

These are briefly presented below:

1. Population is necessarily limited by means of subsistence (food supply). According to Malthus in a country the size of population depends on its food production. Greater the food production, larger would be the size of population, which a country can support and smaller the food production then the country would be in a position to support smaller population only.
2. The power of population is infinitely greater than the power in the earth to produce subsistence for men. He further adds that population growth always overtakes food production, since agricultural production is constrained by the law of diminishing returns. This prevents the food production to grow as faster as that of population. As such, there is no limit to the growth of population.
3. Population increases in geometric progression, whereas food production increases in arithmetic progression. This means that population tends to grow in quick geometric progression i.e., 1, 2, 4, 8, 16, 32, etc., while,

food production tends to grow in arithmetic progression i.e., 1, 2, 3, 4, 5, 6, etc. This implies that population doubles in every 25 years.

4. Population always increases, when the means of subsistence increase, unless it is prevented by some powerful checks. When the food production of a nation increases, the tendency is that it encourages people to have more children and consequently it leads to large families. After certain time, the population would become excessive relative to the food production and the per capita availability of food decreases.
5. There are two types of checks, which can keep population on a level with the means of subsistence viz., preventive checks and positive checks.
   a. **Preventive checks:** These are man – initiated checks to keep the population under control. They aim at decreasing the birth rate. These checks are: 1. celibacy 2. late marriage 3. moral restraints, etc.
   b. **Positive checks:** These are the checks caused by the nature when man fails to take control of the situation. These checks cause the reduction of excess population and thereby bring an equilibrium between demand and supply. We have often the famines, epidemics, wars, floods, earthquakes, etc. These positive checks arc also called as natural checks, since they are caused by nature.

Criticism of Malthusian Theory of Population

This theory was criticized by many economists on several grounds. Some of the important ones are presented below:

1. Presenting the mathematical precision for population growth and food production was objected because as these ratios are found to be unrealistic. There were no instances in the world, where this trend of population growth and food production recorded and the case of doubling of population in every 25 years.
2. Malthus did not foresee the scientific advances that are bound to come in agricultural production, even in the presence of operation of law of diminishing returns.
3. He did not consider total production of nation but confined to agricultural production alone while presenting his theory. In fact it is total production of a country which gives the true picture of its economic position. Consider the example of Great Britain. It was not self – sufficient in agricultural production but it could make great progress through its industrial production. Less agricultural production cannot make the country to be called over – population.

4. It was viewed that increase in population would cause greater demand for food grains, ignoring its contribution in the production of goods and services. Further it was criticized that increase in population in an over – populated country is a matter of serious concern, as it imposes heavy strain on the limited resources of the nation. In respect of an under populated country, increase in population is a welcome sign and it helps to raise economic growth and per capita income
5. Malthus also failed to view that the education and civilization would transform the people to have smaller families. Hence, there would be no danger of over population.
6. Natural calamities which are infact the acts of nature are commonly found everywhere regardless of whether a particular country is over populated or under – populated. So, the statement that natural calamities would occur only in the over populated countries to reduce population is not true.

17.2. Optimum Theory of Population

Prof. Sidgwick gave the foundation of the optimum theory in his principles of political economy. It was later developed by Edwin Cannon. It is also called as the modern theory of population.

17.2.1. Definitions of Optimum Population

1. It generally refers to that size of population which provides maximum income per head at a given amount of resources and technology.
2. Optimum population is that population which produces maximum economic welfare (Carr – Saunders).
3. Optimum population is that which gives the maximum income per head (Dalton).
4. Optimum population in a country ensures 1) best possible utilization of all resources; and 2) highest per capita income. More specifically, optimum population is the right size of population that is most desirable in a country consistent with its supply of resources.

Under Population

If the population of a country is below optimum size i.e., below what it ought to be, the country is said to be under – populated. In such a case the per capita income will not be the highest, as the population is insufficient to use the available resources (both natural and capital) of the country efficiently. The resources are left unharnessed to their optimum level.

Over Population

If the population of a country is in excess of optimum level, the country is said to be over populated. Since the resources are insufficient in relation to the population, the per capita income will not be the highest. Gainful employment is not available to people in view of the insufficiency of resources and requisite technology.

When we say optimum population, it is not fixed for all times. It keeps on changing with the development of technology and growth of capital.

In figure, population is measured on X – axis and output per capita on Y – axis. It is observed that output per capita increases with every increase in population till OQ is reached. At this level of population (optimum population) the per capita output is the highest and is equal to QP. Any further increase of population beyond OQ leads to reduction of output per capita. If the actual population of a country is less than optimum population (OQ), it is under populated and if it is more it is over populated.

Dalton's Formula for Maladjustment

Dalton's maladjustment means the extent of deviation of population from optimum size of population. To measure maladjustment, Dalton gave the following formula.

$$M = \frac{A - O}{O}$$

Where,

M = Maladjustment

A = Actual population

O = Optimum population

A positive 'M' indicates that the country is over – populated.

A negative 'M' indicates that the country is under – populated.

A zero value of 'M' indicates that the actual population is equivalent to optimum population.

17.3. Malthusian Theory of Population Vs Optimum Theory of Population

1. Malthusian theory is based on the relationship between food production and the size of population, while modern theory is based on the relationship between total production of a country and the size of population.

2. Malthusian theory is more a pessimistic theory, while optimum theory is an optimistic one.
3. Malthusian theory has a limitation in its application as it is applicable to over populated countries only, whereas the optimum theory is applicable universally.

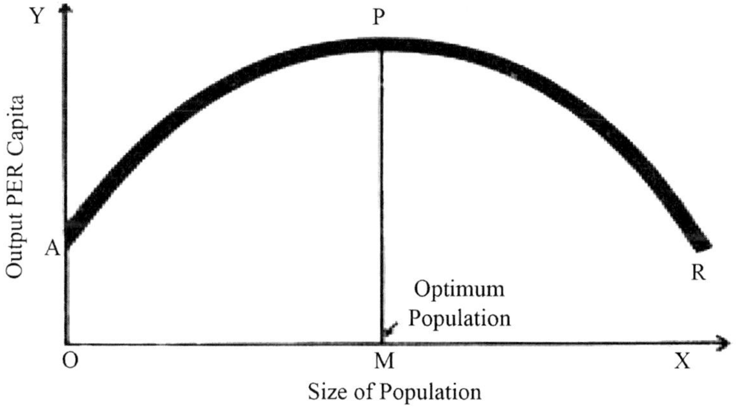

Under, Over, Optimum Population

17.4. Natural and Socio – economic Determinants

Natural Factors

The availability of resources plays a crucial role in determining population growth. When resources are abundant, populations can expand at a geometric or exponential rate. However, as resources become scarce, the growth rate slows down and eventually stabilizes, a phenomenon known as **logistic population growth**. Population growth stops when populations reach a maximum size called the carrying capacity, the number of individuals of a particular population that the environment can support. Population growth is a function both of per capita growth rates and population size.

The environment limits population growth by changing birth and death rates. The factors affecting population size and growth include biotic factors such as food, disease, competitors, and predators and abiotic factors such as rainfall, floods, and temperature. Because the effects of biotic factors, such as disease and predation, are often influenced by population density, biotic factors are often referred to as density-dependent factors. Meanwhile, abiotic factors such as floods and extreme temperature can exert their influences independently of population density and so are often called density- independent factors.

Socio – economic Factors

The socio - economic factors play an crucial role in the growth of population. The socioeconomic factors which affects the growth of population are industrialization, education, religious beliefs, marriage, social status, family structure, health care, nutritional status etc.

There is an inverse relationship with the industrial growth and the rate of population growth. The developed or industrialized countries have less growth of the population. They are mostly stable. The zero growth occurs in Germany and around 1 percent growth occurs in America and France. In Austria there is a negative growth. But in the developing countries there has been an increase in the growth of population. They show a direct relationship.

The education shows an inverse relationship with the rate of population growth. The developed or industrialized countries which have a high literacy rates show less growth of the population. But it is not the only criteria which define the rate of growth of population. In some states like Kerala the literacy rate is very high but they are thickly populated also. There are few religious beliefs which prevent the people to undergo family planning. In such religion dominated countries the population will continue to rise. This occurs despite the higher literacy rates and economic growth. It occurs in the United Arab Emirates and Saudi Arabia. They have a very high population growth rate.

The women can give rise to offspring mainly from the age 15 to 45. If she gets married late naturally the chances of giving birth to more offspring will reduce. It is common in the industrialized countries. The women marry late but in the developing countries the women marry very early around 15 to 20 years of age.

The social status of women is inversely related to the rate of population growth. Women with higher social status tend to marry at a later age. Additionally, family structure and child labor also plays a crucial role in population growth, as families relying on children for income tend to have more children, viewing them as financial contributors.

The health care shows a direct relationship with the rate of population growth. The better is the health care system less is the mortality rate and higher is the natality rate. The families with the gainful employment show low mortality. It decreases the incidence with the large number of children. A well maintained diet helps to reduce the mortality.

The sources of entertainment also play an important role in the growth of population. They keep a routine check on the population. More are the sources of entertainment and lesser are the chances of high natality. The population education shows an inverse relationship with the rate of population growth. The better is the population education the lesser is the growth of population.

17.5 National Population Policy (NPP) 2000

1. **The Immediate Objective:** The immediate objective is to meet the unmet needs for contraception, healthcare infrastructure, and medical personnel while ensuring the integrated delivery of essential reproductive and child healthcare services.
2. **The Medium Term Objective:** The medium term objective is to bring the Total Fertility Rate (TFR) to replacement level by 2010 through vigorous implementation in inter-sectorial operational strategies.
3. **The Long Term Objective:** The long-term objective is to attain a stable population by 2045, aligning with the needs of sustainable economic growth, social development, and environmental protection.

Targets: The following are the targets of National Population Policy:

1. Achieve zero growth rate of population by 2045.
2. Reduce infant mortality rate of below 30 per thousand live births.
3. Reduce maternal mortality ratio of below 100 per 1, 00,000 live births.
4. Reduce birth rate to 21 per 1000 by 2010.
5. Reduce total fertility rate (TFR) to 2.1 by 2010

As a result of the initiatives of the Government, the country's Total Fertility Rate (TFR) has declined from 2.7 in 2006 to 2.2 in 2016. The Crude Birth Rate has declined from 23.8 in 2005 to 20.8 and 24 states/UTs have already achieved the replacement level TFR of 2.1 or less out of 36 states/UTs.

National Socio-Demographic Goals for 2010

To fulfil these objectives and targets, National Socio-Demographic goals have been formulated which in each case are to be achieved by the year 2010.

They are as follows

Ensure free and compulsory education up to the age of 14 while reducing dropout rates at both primary and secondary levels to below 20% for boys and girls.

Address the unmet demands for essential reproductive and child health services, including necessary supplies and infrastructure.

Achieve universal immunization of children against all vaccine-preventable diseases.

Encourage delayed marriage for girls, ensuring it does not occur before 18 years of age and preferably after 20 years.

Implement effective measures to prevent and control communicable diseases.

Provide universal access to information, counseling, and services related to fertility regulation and contraception, offering a diverse range of choices.

Ensure that at least 80% of deliveries occur in healthcare institutions and that 100% of births are attended by trained personnel.

Achieve complete registration of births, marriages, and pregnancies.

Integrate Indian Systems of Medicine (ISM) into reproductive and child health services to enhance outreach at the household level.

Curb the spread of Acquired Immunodeficiency Syndrome (AIDS) while strengthening the integration of Reproductive Tract Infection (RTI) and Sexually Transmitted Infection (STI) management within the National AIDS Control framework.

Foster convergence among related social sector programs to make family welfare initiatives more people-centric.

Actively promote the small family norm to achieve replacement-level Total Fertility Rate (TFR).

Implementation of NPP, 2000: National Commission on Population

In pursuance of NPP, 2000, the Central Government has set up a National Commission on Population (NCP) on 11 May, 2000. It is presided over by the Prime Minister, with the Chief Ministers of all States and UTs and the Central Minister-in-charge of concerned Central Ministries and Departments, reputed demographers, public health professionals and non-government organisations as members. State Level Commissions on Population presided over by the Chief Minister have been set up with the objective of ensuring implementation of the NPP.

The functions of the Commission are

(i) To oversee, evaluate, and guide the implementation of the NPP to ensure the achievement of its established goals;

(ii) To enhance coordination among health, education, environmental, and development programs to accelerate population stabilization;

(iii) To foster inter-sectoral coordination in the planning and execution of programs through various agencies at both the central and state levels and

(iv) To establish a strong public engagement program to support this national initiative.

18

Money

18.1. Meaning

When the human civilization was not developed, people used to exchange those goods which they produced for those which others produced. Such an act of exchanging goods for goods is called barter. But as the years rolled by and when the social organization became more complex, barter system was found to be not practicable. The following are the main difficulties which were found in the barter system.

1. Double coincidence of wants
2. Lack of a standard unit of account
3. Impossibility of subdivision of goods
4. Lack of information
5. Production of large and very costly goods not feasible

The difficulties in barter system were replaced with the introduction of money. Money has been defined as the medium of exchange. According to Robertson money is defined as "Anything which is widely acceptable in discharge of obligations". The different stages in the development of money are as follows.

1. **Commodity Money:** The earliest form of money consisted of goods like rice, wheat, cattle, skins, elephant tusks etc. These were accepted as they were all desired by all the people.
2. **Metallic Money:** As the civilization advanced, people found it difficult to carry on the exchange transaction with commodities, as they were found to be very inconvenient. Commodity money gave way for the metals to be used as money. These metals include gold, silver, copper, bronze, etc. From the beginning of their introduction, Government kept the right to issue coins and certify their weight and quality. Metals were converted into coins for this purpose.
3. **Paper Money:** Paper money is introduced to supplement the metallic money. When paper money was introduced, it was backed up by exactly equal amount of gold or silver kept in reserve by the issuing authority.

But now paper money is not backed up by metals like gold and silver, but only proportional reserves are maintained. Their issue rests more on people's confidence on the issuing authority. Such a currency is called fiduciary issue and Indian currency largely is of fiduciary issue.

4. **Bank Money:** Paper money has been supplemented or at times replaced by bank money. It refers to the bank deposits. Deposits can be converted into money by the depositors through cheques.

18.2. Kinds of Money

The main kinds of money are (1) Metallic money and (2) Paper money. These are further divided into standard money and token money.

1. Standard Money: For such type of money, intrinsic value (real value) is equal to face value (the value written on the coin). It is subjected to free coinage. The coins are made of gold and/ or silver. As such, no country has such a money in circulation.
2. Token Money: This money is made up of cheaper metal. Its face value is greater than its intrinsic value. The rupee is a standard unit of money in India, but its face value is greater than its real value and also it is not subjected to free coinage. It is a mixture of standard and token money.

18.3. Characteristics of Money: Following are the characteristics of money.

1. **Cognoscibility:** The medium used, as money should be easily recognized by one and all. Keeping this in view, the citizens of a nation give value to their respective currencies, issued by monetary authorities. In India the quantum of currency and its value are determined by RBI and Ministry of Finance.
2. **Utility:** When money is deposited by the public in different financing institutions, they will get different interest rates. This is due to the fact that money receiving agency (borrowing agency) will have different time utilities for money. In other words, they use the money for the best alternative and accordingly pay the interest to the lenders, depending on the need. Similarly money will have possession utilities and place utilities also.
3. **Portability:** It should facilitate easy carrying from one place to another without expense or inconvenience to the individual user. In other words, the bulkiness, weight and other inconveniences in the transactions are reduced with the help of currencies of different denominations, such as Rs. 5, Rs. 10, Rs. 20, Rs. 50, Rs. 100, Rs. 500 and Rs. 1000 notes.

4. **Durability:** Coins are more durable than the paper currencies. Particularly, currencies of lower denominations viz., 10 paise, 25 paise, 50 paise, one rupee and 5 rupees are being in circulation in the form of coins in order to provide durability. Similarly keeping the same purpose in view, the standard paper is used for printing currency notes.
5. **Indestructibility:** In the normal usage the coins should not get disfigured easily and the paper currency should not get torn easily in the circulation.
6. **Stability:** The value of money should not be changing. It should be more stable. For this to achieve there is need to eliminate inflation in the economy.
7. **Homogeneity:** All coins of the same metal should be as identified as possible with regard to quality and weights. Similarly notes should be printed with the same quality paper with utmost caution and use of sophisticated machinery, otherwise fake notes come into circulation and cause inflation.
8. **Universal Acceptability:** The value of the currency issued by monetary authority in the country should be recognized uniformly in all the states of the nation. Such currency of the nation will be accepted internationally also, provided the currency follows the norms of international monetary authority.

18.4. Functions of Money: Money performs five important functions

1. **Medium of Exchange:** Money facilitates the buying and selling of goods and services as a medium of exchange.
2. **A unit of account:** Money is used as the measure of value of all goods and services. Rupee is the monetary unit in India. The value of all goods and services is expressed in rupees.
3. **Standard of Deferred Payments:** Money facilitates the settlement of debts and future transactions without any risk.
4. **Store of value:** Money is a form of holding wealth. If one feels that the available money is in excess of his requirements it is convenient to save and use it as and when the need arises.
5. **Transferable:** It facilitates the easy transfer of value. The disposal and purchase of assets can be done very easily with money.

18.5. Money Supply

The supply of money conforms to the '*stock*' concept and not the '*flow*' concept. Just as the demand for money is the demand for money to hold, similarly, the supply of money means the supply of money to hold. Money must always be held by someone, otherwise it cannot exist. Hence, the supply of money means the sum total of all the forms of money which are held by a community at any given moment.

The stock of money, which constitutes the supply of it, constitutes of (a) metallic money or coins (b) currency notes issued by the currency authority of the country whether the Central bank or the government and (c) chequable bank deposits. In old times, the coins formed the bulk of money supply of the country. Later, the currency notes eclipsed the metallic currency and now the bank deposits in current account withdrawable by cheques have overwhelmed all other forms of money. In modern times, the supply of money really means the chequable bank deposits.

The modern economists include in money stock not only currency or cash balances and demand deposits in banks together called $M_{1.}$ In addition to the items of M_1, the concept of money supply M_2 includes savings deposits with the post office savings banks. M_3 is a broad concept of money supply. In addition to the items of money supply included in measure M_1, in money supply M_3 time deposits with the banks are also included. The measure M_4 of money supply includes not only all the items of M_3 but also the total deposits with the post office savings organization.

The total supply of money in a country, by and large, depends on the credit control policies pursued by the banking system of the country.

18.6. Inflation

In economics, **inflation** is a rise in the **general price level** of goods and services in an economy over a period of time.

When the price level increases, each unit of currency can purchase fewer goods and services. As a result, annual inflation leads to a decline in the purchasing power of money, reducing its real value as an internal medium of exchange within the economy.

18.6.1. Inflation Rate?

The inflation rate represents the pace at which the prices of goods and services rise within an economy. It reflects the overall increase in the general price level over time. Given the vast number of goods and services in an economy, calculating the average price change for all items is impractical. Instead, a sample set or **a basket of goods and services** is used to estimate price fluctuations, providing an indicative measure known as the inflation rate.

18.6.2. Measuring inflation

If the price of 1 kg of wheat increases from Rs. 20 to Rs. 25 over a year without any change in quality, this difference represents inflation. However, a single price change does not indicate overall inflation in an economy. To measure general inflation, the price variations of a broad "basket" of representative goods and services are analyzed. This is where a price index comes into play—it reflects the combined price of multiple goods and services in the basket. The combined price is determined by summing up the weighted average prices of the items in the basket. A weighted price is calculated by multiplying the unit price of an item by the quantity an average consumer purchases. This weighted pricing approach is essential for assessing the impact of individual price changes on overall inflation. These weighted average prices are then used to determine the overall price level.To compare price changes over time more effectively, price indexes typically select a base year and assign it a value of 100. The prices in subsequent years are then expressed relative to this base year, making it easier to track inflation trends.

Inflation measures are frequently adjusted over time to reflect market changes. New products are introduced, older ones become obsolete, product quality evolves, and consumer preferences shift. To stay aligned with these changes, both the selection of goods and services in the "basket" and the weighted prices used in inflation calculations are periodically updated.

Inflation numbers are often seasonally adjusted to account for predictable cyclical price fluctuations. For instance, air conditioner prices typically increase during the summer months. In such cases, seasonal adjustments help isolate these expected variations when measuring inflation.

How does India calculate inflation?

In India, inflation is measured on a weekly basis using the Wholesale Price Index (WPI) to determine the inflation rate in the economy. In contrast, most developed countries rely on the Consumer Price Index (CPI) for inflation calculation.

18.6.3. Wholesale Price Index (WPI)

The Wholesale Price Index (WPI) measures changes in the average price level of goods traded in the wholesale market. First introduced in 1902, it served as a key economic indicator for policymakers. However, by the 1970s, most developed countries had replaced it with the Consumer Price Index (CPI) for a more comprehensive measure of inflation.

In India, at present a total of **697 commodities** are included in the commodity basket in which **Primary articles** contribute 117 items, **Fuel and Power** contribute 16 items, and **Manufactured Products** provide 564 items. The base year is 2011-12.

How is WPI (Wholesale Price Index) calculated in India?

For calculation, WPI for the base year is assumed to be 100. Assume that WPI for the year 1993-94 is considered as the base year. Let's calculate WPI for the year 2009-10 for a particular commodity, say wheat. Assume that the price of a kilogram of wheat in 1993-94 = Rs 7.00 and in 2009-10 = Rs 15.00.

$$\text{WPI of wheat}(2009-10) = \frac{(\text{Price of wheat in}2009-10 - \text{ Price of wheat in}1993-94)}{\text{Price of wheat in}1993-94} \times 100$$

$$= \frac{(15.00-7.00)}{7.00} \times 100$$

$$= 114.28$$

Since WPI for base year is assumed as 100, WPI for 2009-10 will become 100+114.28 = 214.28.

Individual WPI values are calculated for all commodities, and their weighted average is then determined to derive the overall Wholesale Price Index. The weight assigned to each commodity is based on its significance and impact on the economy.

How is inflation rate calculated?

If we have the WPI values of two time zones, say, beginning and end of year, the inflation rate for the year will be, (WPI of end of year – WPI of beginning of year) / WPI of beginning of year x 100. For example, WPI for 1st Jan 2009 was 200 and WPI for 1st Jan 2010 was 210 then inflation rate for the year 2009 is (210-200)/200 x 100 = 5%.

Since WPI data is released weekly, inflation for a specific week—typically representing the annual inflation rate for the one-year period ending in that week—is calculated using the WPI of the given week and the WPI from the corresponding week of the previous year.

18.6.4. Consumer Price Index (CPI)

CPI is a measure estimating the average price of consumer goods and services purchased by households. A consumer price index measures a price change for a constant market basket of goods and services from one period to the next within the same area (city, region, or nation). It is a price index determined by measuring the price of a standard group of goods meant to represent the typical market basket of a typical urban consumer.

Effects of Inflation

Inflation's effects on an economy are manifold and can be simultaneously positive and negative.

Negative effects

1. Decrease in the real value of money and other monetary items over time
2. Uncertainty about future inflation may discourage investment and saving, or may lead to reductions in investment of productive capital and increase savings in non-producing assets. e.g. selling stocks and buying gold.
3. Reduce overall economic productivity rates, as the capital required to retool companies becomes more elusive or expensive.
4. High inflation may lead to shortages of goods if consumers begin hoarding out of concern that prices will increase in the future.

Positive effects

1. Mitigation of economic recessions
2. Debt relief by reducing the real level of debt.

Causes of Inflation

1. A high inflation rate results from an **excessive increase in the money supply**. When the money supply grows at a faster pace than economic growth over a prolonged period, it leads to sustained inflation.
2. Low or moderate inflation can be influenced by fluctuations in the real demand for goods and services, changes in supply levels such as during periods of scarcity as well as an increase in the money supply.
3. Generally **during war** and in the **post-war** period, there will be inflation. This is so because during war, there will be shortage of goods and there may be rationing, control and things like that. So during the post-war years, people who have been forced to save money will spend. That is, demand for all sorts of goods will increase during that period but supply will not increase so fast as that. This leads to inflation. Inflation occurs during war because the one great aim at that time is that of winning the war. Since modern wars are so expensive, the Government has to depend upon created money to finance war. This leads to inflation.

4. And inflation breeds inflation. It means that inflation leads to inflation. During a period of inflation, prices will be high. Since prices are high, workers will demand high wages. High wages result in high costs. High costs in turn lead to high prices. Thus it forms a vicious circle. **Wages force up prices; prices force up wages**. This is the **inflationary spiral.**
5. **Deficit financing** is another cause of inflation. This applies particularly to underdeveloped countries with planned economies.

18.6.4. Kinds of Inflation

There are three major types of inflation

1. **Demand-pull inflation:** Demand-pull Inflation occurs when aggregate demand rises due to increased private and government spending, among other factors. Demand-driven inflation can contribute to faster economic growth, as excess demand and favourable market conditions encourage investment and expansion.

   According to the demand-pull theory, inflation accelerates when aggregate demand surpasses the economy's productive capacity. Any factor that boosts aggregate demand can trigger inflation. However, in the long run, maintaining demand above the economy's productive limits is only possible if the money supply grows at a rate faster than the real economic growth rate.
2. **Cost-push inflation:** This type of inflation is also known as supply shock inflation and occurs due to a decline in aggregate supply (potential output). It can be triggered by factors such as natural disasters or rising input costs. For instance, a sudden drop in oil supply, leading to higher oil prices, can result in cost-push inflation. Businesses that rely on oil as a production input may pass these increased costs on to consumers through higher prices.
3. **Built-in inflation:** This type of inflation is driven by adaptive expectations and is often associated with the "price-wage spiral." As inflation rises, workers may demand higher wages to maintain their purchasing power. In response, businesses pass these increased labor costs onto consumers through higher prices, creating a continuous cycle. Built-in inflation is influenced by past economic trends and is sometimes referred to as "hangover inflation."

18.6.5. Other types of Inflation

Repressed Inflation

Generally price rise results in inflation. However, there can be inflation even without a rise in the price level. This is known as Repressed Inflation. Usually this happens during a war period. On account of many controls and rationing that exist during wartime, prices will be kept under check. But the moment controls are withdrawn, prices will go up. So the real test of inflation is neither an increase in the amount of money nor a rise in prices, but the appearance of **abnormal profits**. Whenever businessmen and producers make huge profits, it is a sign of inflation.

Runaway or Galloping or Hyper – Inflation

This is a serious type of inflation. For example, it was experienced in Germany after World War I and in Hungary and China after World War II. In this situation, prices rise to a very great extent at high speed and high prices have to be paid even for cheap things. And money becomes quite worthless and new currency has to be introduced. This situation is known as galloping inflation or hyper-inflation.

Profit – Push Inflation

Just as trade unions manage to push up wages, oligopolists and monopolists will raise prices more than enough to cover increase in costs with the aim of making monopoly profits.

Controlling inflation

Since inflation has numerous negative effects, governments strive to control it using various methods. Most mainstream economists today advocate for a low, stable rate of inflation, as it can help mitigate the impact of economic recessions. The primary tool for managing inflation is monetary policy, typically overseen by monetary authorities, such as central banks. These institutions regulate the money supply by adjusting interest rates, conducting open market operations, and setting banking reserve requirements to keep inflation low and stable.

Some other measures

1. Increased taxation
2. By reducing government expenditure on capital projects. (In India, this measure has been suggested to check inflation. Many capital projects proposed in our Third Five Year Plan were either suspended or dropped completely.

3. Restrictions on imports.
4. Rationing and
5. Price controls.

Sometimes a "wage freeze' is recommended to check inflation. That is, trade unions will be requested not to ask for an increase in wages during a given period. The success of the above measures in tackling inflation depends upon the efficiency of the government in implementing the measures.

Related definitions

Deflation

Deflation is a state in which the value of money is rising, i.e., prices are falling. **Deflation is the opposite of inflation.** Generally inflation is a period characterized by rising activity and employment. But during deflation, there will be **bad trade** and **unemployment**. During deflation, since prices fall faster than costs, there will be heavy losses for producers and businessmen. There will not be profits in any branch of economic activity. So there will be a fall in investment. This results in unemployment. **Both inflation and deflation are evils**. There is nothing much to choose between them. While rising prices can be checked to some extent by the monetary policy of the government, the latter is of little help in raising the price level during deflation. It does not work. That is why during such periods, modern economists suggest that the State must play an active role in the economic field and step up economic activity by undertaking a series of public works programmes.

Disinflation – a decrease in the rate of inflation

Hyperinflation – an out-of-control inflationary spiral

Stagflation – a combination of inflation, slow economic growth and high unemployment

Reflation – an attempt to raise the general level of prices to counteract deflationary pressures.

19

Economics System

An economy is a human-made system developed or adapted to fulfill societal needs. There are three main types of economic systems namely mixed economy, capitalist economy, and socialist economy. The following are some key features of an economy:

- The type of an economy is determined by the ownership of resources and the means of production.
- Resources or means of production may be privately owned, allowing individuals the freedom to use them for profit, or they may be collectively owned and controlled by the government for the overall welfare of society.
- The three types of economic systems are classified based on the extent of individual freedom and the role of profit motive in each.

19.1. Capitalist Economy

The capitalist, or free-market, economy is the most traditional form, where government involvement in economic activities is minimal.

Main features of a capitalist economy

1. **Private property:** In a capitalist economy, individuals have the right to own property, acquire assets, and utilize them for personal gain. There are no limitations on owning land, machinery, mines, or factories for profit and wealth accumulation.
2. **Freedom of enterprise:** Individuals have the freedom to choose any occupation they wish to pursue. The concept of free enterprise means that businesses are free to acquire resources and utilize them to produce any goods or services. Additionally, firms have the liberty to sell their products in any market of their choice, while workers have the right to select their employer.
3. **Consumer Sovereignty:** In a capitalist economy, consumers are regarded as having the highest authority. They have complete freedom to decide how to allocate their money on goods and services that maximize

their satisfaction. Consumer preferences drive production, as businesses cater to their demands. This principle, known as consumer sovereignty, signifies the unrestricted choice consumers have in the market.

4. **Profit Motive:** In a capitalist system, self-interest serves as the driving force. Entrepreneurs recognize that after compensating all factors of production, they retain any remaining profit or bear any losses. This incentivizes them to maximize profits by reducing costs and boosting revenue. Consequently, a capitalist economy operates efficiently and regulates itself.
5. **Competition:** In a capitalist economy, firms can freely enter and exit the market without restrictions. With multiple producers offering the same good or service, no single firm can earn more than a normal profit. Competition is a key feature of capitalism, ensuring consumer protection from exploitation.
6. **Importance of markets and prices:** Several key features of capitalism, including private property ownership, freedom of choice, profit motive, and competition, enable the efficient operation of the price mechanism. At its core, capitalism is a market-driven economy where the price of every commodity is determined by the forces of supply and demand within the industry.
7. **Absence of government intervention:** In a capitalist or free enterprise economy, government intervention and support are generally unnecessary. The government's primary role is to ensure the smooth and efficient functioning of markets. However, pure capitalism no longer exists in the modern world. Countries like the United States, the United Kingdom, France, Spain, the Netherlands, Australia, and Portugal operate under capitalist economic systems.

19.2. Socialist Economy

In socialist or centrally planned economies, the government has complete ownership and control over all productive resources, ensuring their use for the collective welfare of society. Economic decisions are made by a central planning authority, which oversees production, distribution, and resource allocation.

Main features of a socialist economy

1. **Collective ownership of means of production:** In a socialist economy, the government controls and manages all means of production for the collective benefit of society. Private ownership of production units is

eliminated, preventing individuals from accumulating wealth or passing it down to their heirs. However, individuals are allowed to own durable consumer goods for personal use.

2. **Social Welfare Objective:** The government makes decisions with the goal of maximizing social welfare rather than individual profit. Market forces such as demand and supply have little influence, as economic choices are guided by the objective of societal well-being.
3. **Central Planning:** Economic planning is an essential aspect of a socialist economy. The central planning authority distributes resources based on national priorities and available resources. The government takes full responsibility for making economic decisions related to consumption, production, and investment.
4. **Reduction in Inequalities:** The right to own private property and the law of inheritance are key elements of a capitalist economy. However, they contribute to disparities in income and wealth. A socialist system aims to reduce these inequalities by eliminating these features. However, it is important to recognize that achieving absolute equality in income and wealth is neither feasible nor ideal.
5. **No class conflict**: In a capitalist economy, the interests of workers and company management often diverge, as both seek to maximize their own earnings or profits, leading to class conflicts. In contrast, a socialist economy eliminates such conflicts since everyone is considered a worker, and resources are collectively owned for the benefit of all.

19.3. Mixed Economy

A mixed economy combines the best aspects of capitalism and socialism.

The main characteristics of a mixed economy are as follows

1. **Co-existence of public and private sectors**: The private sector consists of privately owned production units that operate for profit, while the public sector comprises government-owned units focused on social welfare. Economic activities in each sector are typically distinct. To regulate and oversee the private sector, the government implements various measures, including licensing, taxation, pricing regulations, and monetary and fiscal policies.
2. **Individual Freedom:** People participate in economic activities to maximize their personal income. They have the freedom to choose their occupation and consume goods and services as they wish. However, producers are restricted from exploiting consumers and workers.

3. **Economic Planning:** The government formulates long-term plans and defines the roles of the private and public sectors in economic development. While it directly controls the public sector and sets production targets and plans, it also encourages, supports, and subsidizes the private sector to align with national priorities.
4. **Price Mechanism:** Prices play a crucial role in resource allocation. In certain sectors, the government implements administered pricing policies. To support specific target groups, it also provides price subsidies. The primary objective is to enhance public welfare by ensuring that essential goods are accessible to those who cannot afford market prices, either by offering them for free or at subsidized rates.

20

International Trade

20.1. Introduction

- The exchange of goods and services (trade) among countries across national boundaries is called as international trade.
- No Country can be self-sufficient in producing all the goods and services required by it.
- Thus, Countries need to trade to obtain commodities, they cannot produce themselves or they can purchase elsewhere at a lower price.
- The act of selling domestically produced goods to international consumer is known as exportation. India Export Refined Petroleum, Jewellery, Rice, etc.
- The act of purchasing goods from foreigne country in order to sell them domestically is known as importation. India import Crude oil, Coal, Gold, Electronics item etc.

20.2. Why International Trade?

- Countries cannot domestically produced all the goods and services that each individual consumer wants and needs.
- Because each country has different factor of production (Land, Labour, and Capital).
- Each country is endowed with different combination of these factors and therefore each country is capable of producing different combination of goods and services.
- When domestic production is greater than domestic demand for a good, excess production is traded on the international market

20.3. Types of International Trade

a) Bilateral Trade

- Trade done by two countries with each other.
- They enter into agreement to trade specified commodities amongst them.

- For example, country A may agree to trade some raw material with agreement to purchase some other specified item from country B or vice versa.

b) Multi- lateral trade

- Multi- Lateral trade is conducted with many trading countries.
- The same country can trade with a number of other countries.
- The United States-Mexico-Canada Agreement (USMCA) is an example of multilateral trade.

20.4. Benefits of International Trade

- Income Generation (Foreign Currency)
- Exchange of Factors of Production
- Employment Generation
- Effective utilization of Resource
- More choices to consumer
- Rise in Standard of Living
- Economics Growth
- Reduced Domestic Monopoly

21

Balance of Payment

21.1. Meaning

Balance of payments is an accounting statement that provide a systematic record to all the economic transaction, between resident of a country and the rest of the world, in a specific time frame.

21.2. Economic Transaction

1. **Visible Items:** These include all types of physical goods which are imported and exported as they are made of some matter that can be seen, touched, measured.
2. **Invisible Items:** Invisible items of trade refers to all types of services like shipping , banking , etc…these are called invisible goods as they can't be felt , seen ,and measured
3. **Unilateral Items or transfer:** Unilateral transfer include gifts, remittance,etc.. since these transaction donot involve any claims for repayments.
4. **Capital transfer:** Capital transfer relate to capital receipts (through borrowings or sale of assets)and capital payments (through capital repayments or purchase of assets)

21.3. Structure of Balance of Payments

1. Credit side

All inflow or sources of foreign exchange are recorded

2. Debit side

All outflow or uses of foreign exchange are recorded on the debit side.

1. Balanced bop
2. Surplus bop
3. Deficit bop

1. **Balance Bop:** Bop is balance when receipt of foreign exchange is equal to payments of foreign exchange.
2. **Surplus BOP:** BOP is surplus when receipt of foreign exchange is more than payments of foreign exchange.
3. **Deficit BOP:** BOP is deficit when the receipt of foreign exchange is less than payments of foreign exchange.

21.4. Meaning of balance of trade

Balance of trade refers to difference between the amount of export and import of visible item.

BALANCE OF TRADE = EXPORT OF GOODS - IMPORTS OF GOODS

21.4.1. Components of balance of payments

1. Current account

The **current account** is a record of all transactions related to the export and import of goods and services, as well as unilateral transfers, over a specific period.

Components of current accounts are:

(i) **Export and Import of Goods:** Export and Import of Goods (Merchandise Transactions or Visible Trade):

A significant portion of foreign trade transactions involves the export and import of goods, also known as visible trade. Payments made for imported goods are recorded as **debit items** (negative side), while receipts from exported goods are recorded as **credit items** (positive side). The difference between visible exports and imports is referred to as the **balance of trade** (or trade balance)

(ii) **Export and Import of Services:** Export and import of services, also known as invisible trade, involve non-factor services (non-visible items) exchanged between a country's residents and the rest of the world, including 3 main types of services namely shipping, banking, and insurance, where payments made are recorded as debits and receipts as credits.

(iii) **Unilateral or Unrequited Transfers to and from abroad (One sided Transactions):** Unilateral transfers refer to one-way transactions such as gifts, donations, personal remittances, and other transfers made without receiving any service or compensation in return. Receipts of unilateral transfers from the rest of the world are recorded on the credit side, while transfers made to the rest of the world are recorded on the debit side.

(iv) **Income receipts and payments to and from abroad:** Income receipts and payments to and from abroad: It encompasses investment income in the form of interest, rent and profits.

21.4.2. Balance on current account

In the current account, receipts from the export of goods and services, as well as unilateral transfers received, are recorded as credit or positive entries. Conversely, payments for the import of goods and services, along with unilateral transfers made, are recorded as debit or negative entries. The net difference between credit and debit entries is referred to as the balance on the current account.

Surplus in the current account arises when Credit items are more than debit items.

Deficit in current account arises when debit items are more than Credit items

2. Capital account

The capital account of the balance of payments records all transactions between a country's residents and the rest of the world that result in changes to the assets or liabilities of the country's residents or its government.

1. **Private Transaction** - When private sector company receive or give short term or long term loan is known as private transactions. In which loan received will come under credit side and repayment or interest on loan come under debit side.
2. **Official Transaction** – Government of country also take short term and long term loans from international institutions like World bank, IMF tec. Reason could be anything , but it is affecting assets and liabilities.
3. **Foreign Direct Investment-** A foreign direct investment (FDI) is an investment made by a firm or individual in one country into business interests located in another country. Generally, FDI takes place when an investor establishes foreign business operations or acquires foreign business assets in a foreign company.
4. **Investment to and from abroad**
   a. Investments from the rest of the world, such as foreign investments in shares of Indian companies or real estate in India, are recorded on the positive (credit) side, as they bring in foreign exchange.
   b. Investments by Indian residents in foreign companies' shares, real estate abroad, and similar assets are recorded on the negative (debit) side, as they result in an outflow of foreign exchange.

21.4.3. Balance on capital account

In the capital account, receipts of foreign exchange, such as loans from abroad, the sale of assets, or shares of foreign companies, are recorded as credit or positive items. Conversely, payments of foreign exchange, including loan repayments, purchases of assets, or shares in foreign countries, are recorded as debit or negative items. The net difference between credit and debit entries is referred to as the balance on the capital account.

Surplus in the capital account arises when Credit items are more than debit items.

Deficit in capital account arises when debit items are more than Credit items.

Difference between Autonomous and Accommodating items

1. Autonomous item

It refers to those international economic transaction, which take place due to some economic motive such as profit maximization.

i) These items are also known as above line item

ii) Autonomous transaction are independent of the state of BOP accounts.

2. Accommodating items

Accommodating items referred as the transaction that are undertaken to cover deficit or surplus in autonomous transaction i.e. such transaction are determined by net consequences of autonomous transaction…

1. These items are also known as below the line item.
2. Accommodating transaction take place only on capital account .

Deficit in Balance of payment

1. A decline in demand for a country's goods in foreign markets reduces exports, negatively impacting the balance of payments.
2. High inflation- When there is inflation in the domestic economy, foreign goods become relatively cheaper as compared to domestic goods. It increases imports which causes a deficit in the BOP.

3. Import of services-

Underdeveloped countries import services from developed countries for which, they have to pay huge amounts of money. It result in deficit in the BOP.

4. Development Process

Developing countries depend on developed nations for supply of machines, technology and other equipment. This leads to increased levels of imports, thereby, resulting in a deficit in the BOP account.

5. Cyclic fluctuations

When the domestic economy is going through a phase of boom, then domestic production may be unable to satisfy the domestic demand. It leads to a deficit in BOP, due to increase in imports.

Political Factors

1. **Political instability:** Political instability may lead to large capital outflows and reduce the inflows of foreign funds, thus, creating disequilibrium in the BOP.
2. **Policitcal disturbance:** Frequent changes in the government, inadequate support to the government in parliament also discourage inflows of capital. This leads to a deficit due to higher outflows than inflows.
3. Social Factors: Change in taste and preferences- An unfavorable change for the domestic goods leads to a deficit in the balance of payments.

21.4.4. Demonstration effect

When the people of developed countries come in contact with those of advanced countries, they start adopting the foreign pattern of consumption. As a result, imports increases, leading to an adverse balance of payments for underdeveloped countries.

21.4.5. Difference between Balance of Trade Vs Balance of Payments

Basis For Comparison	**Balance of Trade**	**Balance of Payment**
Meaning	Balance of Trade is a statement that captures the country's export and import of goods with the remaining world.	Balance of Payment is a statement that keeps track of all economic transactions done by the country with the remaining world.
Records	Transactions related to goods only.	Transactions related to both goods and services are recorded.
Capital Transfers	Are not included in the Balance of Trade.	Are included in Balance of Payment.
Which is better?	It gives a partial view of the country's economic status.	It gives a clear view of the economic position of the country.
Result	It can be Favourable, Unfavourable or balanced.	Both the receipts and payment sides tallies.
Component	It is a component of Current Account of Balance of Payment.	Current Account and Capital Account.

22

Goods and Services Tax (GST)

22.1. Meaning

GST is a tax imposed on the purchase of goods and services. It is designed to be a single, comprehensive tax that replaces multiple smaller indirect taxes on consumption, such as service tax.

- The taxes are included in the final price and are to be paid by the consumers at point of sale and passed on to the government by the seller.
- The GST is a common tax used by the majority of countries globally.
- It is a unified tax applied to the supply of goods and services from the manufacturer to the final consumers.
- More than 160 developed countries implement this system of taxation.
- The GST is usually taxed at a single rate across the nation.

22.2. Main Features of Goods and Services Tax (GST)

The main features of Goods and Services Tax are as follows:

- **Dual GST-** India has implemented a dual GST system, consisting of two components: Central GST (CGST) and State GST (SGST). The central government collects CGST, while states and union territories collect SGST/UTGST on all supply transactions of goods and services. Following the 101st Constitutional Amendment, both the central government and union territories have the authority to levy taxes simultaneously on the supply of goods and services.
- **Applicable on supply side-** GST is applicable on "supply" of goods or services as against the old concept on the manufacturer of goods or on sale of goods or on provision of services.
- **Destination based taxation-** GST is based on the principle of destination-based consumption taxation as against the present principle of origin-based taxation.
- **GST rates to be mutually decided-** CGST, SGST & IGST are levied at rates to be mutually agreed upon by the center and the states on the recommendation of the GST council.

- **Multiple Rates-** GST was levied at four rates viz. 5%, 12%, 16% and 28%.The list of items that fall under these multiple slabs are worked out by the GST council.

22.3. Legislative Basis of GST

GST got an approval in 2016 and was renumbered in the statute by the Rajya Sabha as the constitution 101st Amendment Act, 2016. In India, the GST bill was first introduced in India in 2014 as the Constitution (122nd Amendment) Bill.

Its provisions are given below:

- CGST to cover Excise duty, service tax etc
- SGST to cover VAT ,luxury tax etc.
- Article 246 A – states have power to tax goods and services.
- Integrated GST to cover Inter-state trade. IGST Per se is not an attack but a system to coordinate state and union taxes.

22.4. GST Council

The 101st Amendment Act of 2016 laid the foundation for implementing a new tax regime, the Goods and Services Tax (GST), in the country. The effective and efficient administration of this tax relies on cooperation and coordination between the central and state governments. To facilitate this consultation process, the amendment mandated the establishment of the Goods and Services Tax Council (GST Council).

- Article 279 A – The amendment inserted a new article in the constitution. This article gives power to the President to constitute a GST council by an order which will govern and administer GST. Its chairman is union finance minister of India with ministers nominated by the state governments as its members.
- The Secretariat of the council is located at New Delhi.
- The union Revenue Secretary acts as the ex officio secretary to the council.
- The GST council is devised in such a way that the center will have 1/3 voting power and the states have 2/3rd.
- The decisions are taken by the 3/4th Majority.
- The union Cabinet also decided to include the chairperson of the Central Board of Excise and Customs (CBEC) as a permanent invitee (non voting) to all proceedings of the council.

22.5. Function of The GST Council

The GST council is required to make recommendation to the center and the states on the following matters:

- The taxes, cesses and surcharges levied by the center, the States and the local bodies that would get merged in GST.
- The goods and services that may be subjected to GST or exempted from GST.
- The rates include flow rates with bands of GST.
- The threshold limit of turnover below with goods and services may be exempted from GST.
- Model GST laws, principles of Levi, apportionment of GST leave it on supplies in the course of inter- state trade or commerce and the principles that govern the place of supply.

22.6. Reforms Brought About by GST

The reforms brought about by GST are as follows:

- **Reduced tax burden:** GST eliminated the 'tax on tax' phenomenon, leading to lower overall tax burden on businesses and consumers.
- **Create a common national market:** By amalgamating a large number of central and state taxes into single tax.
- **Making India products more Competitive:** The introduction of the Goods and Services Tax (GST) has made Indian products more competitive in both domestic and international markets by ensuring the full neutralization of input taxes across the production value chain.
- **Easier to administer:** As the GST is so transparent and self-policing, it would be easier to administer.
- **Mitigation of cascading effect:** GST mitigated ill effects of cascading or double taxation in a major way and paved the way for a common national market.

22.7. Advantages of Goods and Service Tax

The advantages of goods and services tax are as follows:

- Goods and service tax is a transparent tax that produces the number of indirect taxes.
- It benefited people as prices will come down within turn will help companies as consumption will increase.

- GST will not burden registered retailers, eliminating hidden taxes and reducing the cost of doing business.
- Under the current taxation system, separate taxes for goods and services require dividing transaction values between the two, making tax administration more complex and increasing compliance costs.
- In the production and the distribution of goods, services are increasingly used or consumed and vice versa.
- GST will promote transparency and help establish a corruption-free tax administration.
- GST will facilitate the creation of a unified national market in India. It will also encourage foreign investment and strengthen the Make in India campaign.
- Increased reliance on income tax will minimize direct interaction between taxpayers and the tax administration, significantly reducing corruption.
- As states will be able to tax the entire supply chain for manufacturing to retail.
- As a destination-based consumption tax, GST primarily benefits consuming states. It will also enhance the overall investment climate in the country, contributing to the development of states.
- GST will contribute to poverty eradication by creating more employment opportunities and increasing financial resources.
- GST will increase ease of doing business and will also help in reduction and multiplicity of taxes.
- GST will decrease the average tax burden on supply of goods or services and simplify the procedures for registration, returns, funds and tax payment.

22.8. Disadvantages of GST

The disadvantages of GST are as follows:

- Some economists argue that GST in India could adversely affect the real estate market, potentially increasing the cost of new homes by up to 8% and reducing demand by approximately 12%.
- Some experts believe that the Central Goods and Services Tax (CGST) and State Goods and Services Tax (SGST) are merely renamed versions of Central Excise/Service Tax, VAT, and CST. Therefore, they argue that there will be no significant reduction in the number of tax layers.

- The adoption and transition to the new GST system will come with initial challenges and a learning curve for the entire ecosystem.
- The aviation industry will also be impacted, as the current tax on airfares ranges from 6% to 9%. With GST, this rate will exceed 15%, effectively doubling the tax burden.
- Some retail products currently have only a minimal tax applied. With the implementation of GST, garments and clothing may become more expensive.

22.9. Challenges of GST

The challenges of GST are as follows:

- SGST & CGST input credit cannot be cross utilised.
- The manufacturing states will lose revenue on a bigger scale.
- The fiscal autonomy of the states will be diminished.
- The concerns raised by banks and insurance companies over the need for multiple registration under GST.
- The success rate of GST totally depends on the technology, capacity of tax officials and the political consensus to adapt the new requirement.
- The levy of additional cess.

Glossary

- **Agribusiness**: The business of agricultural production, including farming, processing, and distribution.
- **Agricultural Economics**: The study of resource allocation, production, and distribution in the agricultural sector.
- **Balance of Payment**: A record of a country's transactions with the rest of the world.
- **Capital**: Financial assets or resources utilized in the production of goods and services.
- **Commodity**: A raw material or primary agricultural product that can be bought and sold.
- **Consumer's Surplus**: The disparity between what consumers are willing to pay and what they actually pay.
- **Cost**: The expenses incurred in the production process.
- **Crop Rotation**: The practice of growing different crops in succession on the same land to maintain soil fertility.
- **Demand**: The quantity of a product or service that consumers are willing to buy at a given price.
- **Depreciation**: The reduction in the value of an asset over time due to wear and tear.
- **Distribution**: The process of allocating resources or goods among producers, consumers, and other stakeholders.
- **Economic System**: The structure through which a society organizes its production, distribution, and consumption.
- **Economies of Scale**: Cost advantages achieved by increasing the scale of production.
- **Elasticity of Demand**: A metric of how demand for a good changes in response to price changes.
- **Farm Management**: The process of organizing and operating a farm to maximize productivity and profitability.
- **Fixed Costs**: Costs that do not change with the level of production, such as rent or salaries.
- **Goods and Services Tax (GST)**: A value-added tax levied on the supply of goods and services.

- **Gross Domestic Product (GDP)**: The total value of goods and services produced within a country in a specific period.
- **Inflation**: The rate at which the general level of prices for goods and services rises.
- **Input-Output Relationship**: The connection between the quantity of inputs used and the resulting output.
- **International Trade**: The exchange of goods and services across borders.
- **Labor**: Human effort used in the production process.
- **Land**: Natural resources used in agriculture, such as soil, water, and climate.
- **Law of Variable Proportion**: An economic principle stating that varying one input while keeping others constant affects output.
- **Laws of Returns**: Principles describing the relationship between input levels and output in production.
- **Marginal Cost**: The cost of producing one additional unit of a good.
- **Market Equilibrium**: The point where supply and demand are balanced, determining the market price.
- **Money**: A medium of exchange used to facilitate transactions and store value.
- **National Income**: The total income earned by a country's residents, including wages, profits, and rents.
- **Opportunity Cost**: The value of the next best alternative foregone when making a decision.
- **Population**: The number of people living in a specific area, influencing demand and labor supply.
- **Price Elasticity**: A measure of how the quantity demanded or supplied changes with price.
- **Production**: The process of creating goods or services using inputs like land, labor, and capital.
- **Productivity**: The efficiency with which inputs are converted into outputs.
- **Return to Scale**: The rate at which output increases as all inputs are scaled up.
- **Subsidy**: Financial assistance provided by the government to support agricultural activities.

- **Supply**: The quantity of a product that producers are willing to offer at a given price.
- **Sustainability**: Practices that meet current needs without compromising future generations.
- **Tariff**: A tax imposed on imported goods to protect domestic industries.
- **Utility Theory**: A concept explaining how consumers maximize satisfaction from goods and services.
- **Value Chain**: The series of steps involved in producing, processing, and delivering a product to consumers.
- **Yield**: The amount of agricultural produce obtained from a given area of land.

References

Ahuja, H.L., Advanced Economic Theory: Microeconomics Analysis, S. Chand & Company Ltd., New Delhi, 1979.

Barthwal, R.R., Microeconomic Analysis, Wiley Eastern Ltd. New Delhi, 1992.

Castle, E.N. and M.H. Becker., Farm Business Management: The Decision Making Process, The Macmillan Company, New York, 1965, Dhondyal, S.P., Farm Management (an economic analysis), Friends Publications.

Dewett, K.K. and Adarsh Chand., Modern Economic Theory, Shyam Lal Charitable Trust, New Delhi, 1997.

Dewett, K.K. and Varma, J.D., Elementary Economic Theory, S. Chand & Company Ltd., New Delhi, 1985.

Efferson, J. Norman., Principles of Farm Management, McGraw-Hill Book Company, Inc., New York, 1953.

Gail, L. Cramer and Clarence W. Jensen., Agricultural Economics and Agribusiness, John Wiley & Sons, Inc., New York, 1994.

Gupta, G.S., Managerial Economics, Tata McGraw-Hill Publishing Company Ltd, New Delhi, 1990.

Jhingan, M.L, Microeconomic Theory, Vikas Publishing House Pvt. Ltd., New Delhi, 1982.

Johl, S.S. and T.R. Kapur., Fundamentals of Farm Business Management, Kalyani Publishers, Ludhiana, 1987.

Joshi, J.M. and Rajendra Joshi., Microeconomic Theory: An Analytical Approach, Wishwa Prakashan, New Delhi, 1994.

Kahlon, A.S. and Karam Singh., Economics of Farm Management in India: Theory and Practice, Allied Publishers Private Ltd., New Delhi, 1980.

Koutsoyiannis, A., Modern Microeconomics, English Language Book Society/Macmillan, London, 1979.

Paul Loomba, N., Linear Programming: An Introductory Analysis, Tata McGraw-Hill Publishing Company Ltd., New Delhi, 1989.

Prem Kumar Gupta. and D.S. Hira., Operations Research, S. Chand & Company Ltd., New Delhi, 2000.

Richard, W. Leftwich and Ross. D. Eckert., The Price System and Resource Allocation, Holt-Saunders, Japan, 1985.

Robert O' Connor., Principles of Farm Business Analysis and Management, Irish University press, Shannon, Ireland, 1973.

Rout, R.K. A text book of Basic Agricultural Economics. Kalyani Publisher, 2022.

Samuelson, Paul A. and William, D. Nordhaus., Economics, McGraw-Hill Book Company, New York, 1989.

Sankhayan, P.L., Introduction to Farm Management, Tata McGraw-Hill Publishing Company Ltd., New Delhi, 1983.

Seth, M.L., Principles of Economics, Lakshminarayan Agarwal Educational Publish-ers, New Delhi, 1968.
Sharma, A.N. and V.K. Sharma., Elements of Farm Management, Prentice-Hall of India Pvt. Ltd., New Delhi, 1981.
Singh, L.J., Elements of Farm Management Economics, Affiliated East-West Press Private Ltd., New Delhi, 1977.
Stonier, A.W. and Hague Douglas C., A Textbook of Economic Theory, The English Language Book Society and Longman's Green and Company Ltd., London, 1962.
Subba Reddy S., P.S. Ram, T.V.N. Sastry, I.B. Devi, Agricultural Economics. Oxford & IBH Publishing Co. Pvt. Ltd. New Delhi, 2015.
Sundharam, K.P.M. and M.C. Vaish., Microeconomic Theory, S. Chand & Company Ltd., New Delhi, 1977.
Taha Hamdy, A., Operations Research: An Introduction, Macmillan Publishing Com-pany, New York, 1989.
Tewari, D.D. and Katar Singh., Principles of Microeconomics, New Age International (P) Ltd., Publishers, New Delhi, 1996.
William J. Baumol., Economic Theory and Operations Analysis, Prentice-Hall of India Pvt. Ltd., New Delhi, 1978.
Yang, W.Y., Methods of Farm Management Investigations, Food and Agriculture Organisation of the United Nations, Rome, Italy, 1971

Index